Raising Resilient Sons

A Boy Mom's Guide to Building a Strong, Confident, and Emotionally Intelligent Family

Colleen Kessler, EdM

Published in the United States by:
Ulysses Press
P.O. Box 3440
Berkeley, CA 94703
www.ulyssespress.com

ISBN: 978-1-64604-074-2
Library of Congress Control Number: 2020935546

Printed in Canada by Marquis Book Printing
10 9 8 7 6 5 4 3 2 1

Acquisitions editor: Ashten Evans
Managing editor: Claire Chun
Project editor: Claire Sielaff
Editor: Renee Rutledge
Proofreader: Kate St.Clair
Front cover design: Justin Shirley
Cover artwork: © tykcartoon/shutterstock.com
Interior design and layout: what!design @ whatweb.com

To Trevor and Isaac—my strong, confident, and resilient sons.

To Molly and Logan—my strong, confident, and resilient daughters.

To Brian—my support and partner in this adventure of building an emotionally intelligent family.

Contents

Introduction

The spirit is there in every boy; it has to be discovered and brought to life.

—Robert Baden-Powell

I couldn't wait to be a boy mom.

Don't misunderstand me. I love my girls with all my heart, but when I dreamed of having that first baby, I wanted a boy. I imagined mommy-son snuggles, dirty feet, wide-eyed adoration, and all the stereotypical things that went along with being part of the "boy mom" tribe.

I envisioned a big brother to his younger siblings, standing up to any injustices. That whole "I can tease and pick on them all I want, but watch out to anyone else who tries that!" idea of a protector, teaser, prankster, cuddler, and all-around leader of the pack of small beings I was bound to be blessed with.

My boys would be sensitive and smart. They wouldn't be too rough. I wasn't going to conform to the stereotypes and only buy the "boyish toys." No guns and swords and weapons, either...oh no! *My* boys wouldn't be violent. They'd be calm and creative, fun and loving, embodying the best of the rough-and-tumble boy life, but with a soft side. I would give them trucks and cars to play with, and baby dolls to love. My sons would learn to nurture and protect while being rugged and industrious.

Are you laughing at Past Me yet?

There are so many books and articles that caution young moms about raising overly masculine and aggressive boys. They implore parents to teach their sons to be calmer, quieter, and more compliant than the impulsive boys who yank pigtails– those who fall under the "boys will be boys" stereotype.

I tried being that enlightened mom with my firstborn. I rocked him and cuddled him and read him sweet stories. He'd take them in, snuggle back, and then grab fistfuls of the dog's fur as she passed. He was a fitful sleeper and destroyer of all block towers in his path.

I'll never forget sitting at a coffee shop with some of my work friends. We'd formed a prayer group of sorts, where we read books about faith, parenting, mothering, or being a woman, and we'd meet once a week to discuss the next chapter, talk about being new moms, and care for each other. Two of my friends' sweet little girls are the same age as my eighteen-month-old little boy. Those toddler girls sat in the wooden restaurant high chairs with their coloring, crafts, neatly cut-up snacks, and sippy cups while their mamas chatted at the table.

My toddler boy drove cars beneath the table around our feet, crashing them together and making sound effects, his coloring books forgotten or used as tunnels and ramps. He wove in and out of the tables in our little deserted section of the coffee shop, discarding the coloring sheet I tried giving him. He pulled away as I tried to wipe the smeared icing off his face, then crashed, eye first, into the corner of the table next to us, letting out a wail that could be heard two cities away.

That little boy did not want to sit and color. He never stopped moving. He didn't gravitate toward the stuffed animals, games, and sorting toys I had strategically placed around our home. Well, unless it was to topple things, wrestle with the stuffed animals, or fashion the sorting toys into weapons to protect me from invaders. He was my knight in armor, ready to defend my life and my honor at a moment's notice.

He climbed, jumped, grabbed, and investigated the most dangerous things he could possibly find. If I turned my back for a minute, he'd be gone. The day after that embarrassing coffee date I mentioned, I was cleaning up some toys in the family room, where he was bouncing up and down to the music from a Baby Einstein video. I dragged the box down the hallway to the back room in our tiny 1,100-square-foot house and came back minutes later to an empty family room, music still playing.

I looked under furniture and behind plants, then heard water running upstairs in our only bathroom with a tub. I ran up the narrow, steep stairs of our little 1850s farmhouse to find him standing in the tub, diaper and shorts in a soggy heap on the bathroom floor, his onesie dangling and dripping, half on and half off. His black eye was glistening as water droplets sprayed his face from the detachable shower head he pointed at himself.

Using what he'd learned from *Baby Signs*, he signed "water" and grinned proudly. I sighed and helped him take his onesie the rest of the way off and sat on the closed toilet seat, breathing slowly while he occupied himself in the shower for a few minutes before, inevitably, he was off again.

Dr. Leonard Sax, author of *Why Gender Matters*, explains that despite our planning and plotting, boys and girls will always be different, and parents, teachers, and caregivers would do well to learn about those differences so they can help kids reach their full potential. One of our biggest challenges as parents is figuring out what those differences are, seeing how they apply to our own sons, and then using that knowledge to be the amazing parents we are meant to be.

In his book, Dr. Sax shares how some of the things we typically associate with boys–distraction, hyperactivity, impulsivity, physical aggression–are actually misunderstood pieces of their biology that, when properly addressed, can help us unlock their potential.

Dr. Michael C. Reichert, author of *How to Raise a Boy*, tells us that most parenting books send messages about boys that fall into two camps: (1) that boys are biologically driven to rambunctious play, aggression, and risk-taking or (2) that they are innocent victims of social oppression, playing into our preconceived gendered norms. What's missing from these discussions, Dr. Reichert goes on to say, is that lovely, imaginative, and inspiring part played by a boy's dreams, goals, nature, and psychology. Who they're meant to be. What they're born for.

Our boys are neither victims of biology *nor* the social ecology. But they have gotten the short end of the stick for too long. They're different, and that's okay. It's meant to be. It's our job, mamas, to help them harness their energy *and* grow in strength and empathy too.

As a boy mom today, I worry for my sons. I worry that they're being discriminated against for how they're biologically and neurologically wired. That they're mistrusted just because they're male. That's not fair or right. We need to fight back, boy moms. We need to stand up for our sons now, and be proud of all that comes along with being boy moms. We can help our boys grow up to be men of integrity, compassion, confidence, and fairness. We can nurture their emotional intelligence so they can truly understand another person's perspective, think critically, and stand up for what is right. And we can equip them to be strong enough to bounce back from trauma, displaying a lifelong resiliency that will help them be amazing friends, spouses, and fathers in their own time.

In an article entitled "What Happened After My 13-Year-Old Son Joined the Alt-Right," published in the *Washingtonian* in 2019, the author described a dark spiral her young teen took after a girl at school made what she later admitted was a false sexual harassment claim against him. He felt lost and let down by the administrator and guidance counselor, who were supposed to be there for him. The story ends with her son coming out of that dark time, but not before being exposed to a kind of underbelly in cyberspace and a loss of the innocence he'd had before that accusation. Scary stuff, mamas.

According to the article, a school administrator made a comment to the boy and his parents that, as a father of daughters, it was his job to believe and protect the girls under his care at the school. He admitted in that board room that he took the girl's word over the boy's. The accused boy's assertion that he hadn't done or said anything to the girl, who admitted later that she'd made it all up because she wanted him to like her, seemed to mean less to that administrator because he was male. That administrator told the boy's parents that it was his "primary duty, as a school official and as a father of daughters, to believe and to protect the girls under his care." But at what cost? And how do we raise our sons to want to stand up–for themselves and others–if the world around them isn't supportive of them simply because they're boys?

What message does this send to our sons? That they need to be perfect and completely above reproach at all times simply because they are male? It's just not fair to put that kind of pressure on a young boy. Childhood is a time when kids are supposed to make mistakes so they can learn from them and grow while they're surrounded by people–at home, school, sports, churches, and homeschool co-ops if they aren't in a traditional homeschool setting–who love them and have their best interests at heart. It's a time when boys and girls mess up equally. Both boys and girls do impulsive things, say things they don't mean to get someone in trouble, or push the envelope. It's our duty to believe all kids and shepherd them toward building resiliency, integrity, and emotional intelligence. It's our duty to stand up, boy moms, and protect our sons while raising them to be good, strong men.

I'm the proud mom to two sons. My boys are quirky, creative, fun, impulsive, crazy smart, and often endearingly absentminded. I'm also the proud mom of two daughters, so I understand the instinct to protect them above all. I've found myself being harder on my oldest son than his sister, simply because he is stronger than her and "should protect her."

I'm a work in progress. What I do know is this–there is a lot of information out there bombarding us as parents, and more specifically, as boy moms. Books on how to raise the best boys possible, on parenting confident kids, resilient kids, emotionally intelligent kids, kids with ADHD, gifted kids, kids with special needs, and everything in between. I've read an exhausting number of them. (I've shared information about some of my favorites in the resource section of this book and you can find clickable links to them and loads of other resources on the website for this book, RaisingResilientSons.com.)

It's easy to become overwhelmed. Like me, you're probably a mama of boys who feel passionately that they are who they are meant to be. Their brains are wired for adventure. They're meant to be strong and confident, protectors of the innocent, champions of the persecuted. They're meant to fight for justice and love deeply. To forge new trails, discover new and better ways of doing things, and be mindful, caring, and connected to their people and their world.

In this book, we'll explore the ideas behind resiliency and emotional intelligence, and how they relate to our precious sons. I'm a hands-on mama, with a love for research and a passion for distilling reams of information down to pragmatic and applicable ideas, so you'll walk away from this book with a slew of actionable tips and strategies for meeting your sons right where they are–from teeny tots to towering teens–to build the family of your dreams. I'll make sure of it, and I'll be right there with you every step of the way.

Take a deep breath, grab a cup of coffee (or glass of wine) and some chocolate. Let's get started, mama!

Part One

Getting Ready

*Character cannot be developed
in ease and quiet. Only through
experience of trial and suffering can
the soul be strengthened, ambition
inspired, and success achieved.*

— Helen Keller

Miles was an adorable boy. Blond hair, blue eyes, and a little dimple in his cheek when he smiled his slightly mischievous grin. From the time he was small he did all the boy things–T-Ball, soccer, basketball–and he excelled. He was popular when he started school, was always surrounded by lots of kids on the playground, and had a full calendar of birthday parties, playdates, and sporting events to attend. His mom talked proudly about how well liked he was with neighbors, friends, and family.

But Miles wasn't the greatest student. He did well enough to pass just under the radar, though he was often in trouble for talking too much in class. In high school he played sports and dated equally popular girls, and fell further behind. He didn't really care, though, because he had figured out how to game the system, and he was really well versed in cheating. His parents made sure he had the right "stuff" to fit in with the kids he hung around–a car, great clothes, a cell phone, and they were there for every game and awards night. He got into trouble here and there–for cheating, lying, or sneaking out–and his dad would rage, then his mom would step in and calm her husband down, reminding him how much pressure Miles was under. She always fixed things for Miles.

When he got to college, Miles struggled. His mom wasn't there with him, and he had trouble managing his time well. His grades, never great to begin with, plummeted. He started skipping class because it was easier than facing his professors. By the third quarter of his freshman year, he had dropped out. He moved back home and took a part-time job at the office where his mother worked.

Miles's mom had the same dream that most of us have–to raise sons who live happy, worry-free, and painless lives. We'd all love to raise sons who grow up with minimal inconveniences and no broken bones, lost games, bad grades, drug experiments, or relational indiscretions. We'd love to live in a world where our boys didn't have to worry about peer pressure, bullying, sickness, fights, poverty, or crime. Boy moms like you and me imagine that we can protect our sons from hurt, heartache, loss, and misfortune.

But the truth is, we'd be doing our sons a disservice if we isolated them from all conflict. Miles's mom had his best interests at the center of her heart, but by taking too much control, she robbed him of the opportunity to learn resilience and to build his emotional intelligence so that he could be successful on his own merits.

If our sons don't face disappointments and challenges, they will never have the satisfaction of rising to the occasion and triumphing over adversity. They won't begin to understand how strong they truly are and how much they can do, even in the middle of a tough situation. If our sons don't face challenges, they won't have the chance to bask in success or revel in the joy of accomplishment.

None of us really want our kiddos to face troubled times, but we need to be realistic when it comes to parenting. There will be problems. Our goal, instead, should be to raise resilient sons, those who can handle the everyday bumps in the road and can bounce back when bad things happen. We want to help them develop thick, deep roots that will allow them to stretch and grow tall and spread their branches far.

To help them without enabling weakness, we need to help our sons build that bounce-back spirit that gets them through tough times and sees them coming out stronger on the other side. We also need to mentor them to develop emotional intelligence and self-regulation. When they understand their own emotions and reactions to things and can control those reactions well, all while understanding that others have emotional needs too, they can develop maturity and propel themselves toward success.

Finally, we need to take care of ourselves, mama. It is very important to raise strong sons, but we are no good to our families if we're huddled on the couch depleted. That saying *you can't pour from an empty vessel* is cliché because it's true. If you have nothing left to give, emotionally, you are not modeling for your sons how you self-regulate. And, mama, what kind of example are we setting for our sons when we do it all and burn ourselves out to the point that they never want to have a family of their own because you just don't seem to be having any fun?

You can do this, though. You can raise resilient and emotionally intelligent sons, all while taking care of yourself in the process. I promise.

Chapter One

Resiliency

Courage doesn't always roar.
Sometimes courage is the little
voice at the end of the day that
says "I'll try again tomorrow."

—Mary Anne Radmacher

Cristy became a full-time parent to Jay when she married his dad. A nine-year-old who was a good student in school, he seemed exceptionally bright to her. She didn't struggle with him over academic issues until he reached the ninth grade.

According to their family rules, school was Jay's job, and he couldn't take part in any extracurricular activities if he didn't do his job. At the end of Jay's ninth-grade year, they were stunned to hear that he would not pass algebra. He was always a good math student, but according to his teacher, he didn't finish his schoolwork or study for his tests. The teacher explained that he had been warned that if he wanted to move up to the next level of math in tenth grade, he had to take algebra in summer school. The warning had made no difference to Jay. He flunked. Cristy and his dad signed him up for the six-week online summer school class for algebra.

He started his class, and then Jay heard the hard news; his youth group service camp was in three weeks. In this week-long camp put together by his youth group, students stayed together in Cincinnati and did service projects for the community. He had been so excited to finally be old enough to attend. Unfortunately, his service camp was in the middle of summer school, and there was that pesky family rule about academics trumping activities.

Jay sat down and started his algebra. He knew he wouldn't go to service camp unless he finished summer school. Day after day, he sat down and watched the lessons and did the assignments. At the end of two weeks, Cristy was notified by email that Jay had taken all his exams, finished his final, and that all the grading had been completed. He scored an A–finishing a six-week algebra course in two weeks!

Grit and determination helped this previously unmotivated young man accomplish what no teacher could get him to do. And Jay went to service camp a week later.

Mental capabilities like determination, grit, motivation, drive, self-worth, kindness, and confidence are what make our sons resilient, able to cope with stress and push through even the most difficult challenges in the pursuit of their goals. Resiliency fosters well-being in our sons–a sense of love, happiness, peace, and calm. And as our boys feel more rooted and happier, their well-being increases, giving rise to greater resilience, which then floods them with more happiness. It's an unending circle of growth that makes our kids stronger and more emotionally sound every day.

They key is knowing how to strengthen those roots in our boys so that they can turn those fleeting challenges and disappointments into lasting inner strength and resilience. This relies on a little bit of neurology knowledge and something called positive neuroplasticity.

Forging Positive Pathways

When I talk to kids about their brains, I keep it simple. I use terms like "wiring" and "mental muscle," and so I'll do that here too. Our kiddos' brains are a work in progress, so it's never too late to help them form new connections or to, quite literally, change the way their brains react to things for the better. Explain to your sons that when they repeatedly stimulate a pathway, they strengthen it. They can learn to be calmer, more confident, and more empathetic in the same way they learn anything else: *by practicing*.

The human brain is designed to be changed by human experiences. Our sons become what their attention rests on. It's up to us to give them the opportunity to practice–and notice–those situations that strengthen their resiliency.

Mindfulness helps our kids develop a growth mindset approach to building resiliency. Resilient people see opportunities instead of setbacks. They don't look for problems, but they know that when they face them, they'll grow in positive ways from the experience. We want our sons to see challenges as opportunities for growth because life is a series of ups and downs, and the ups are so much richer when we approach the downs with a positive spin.

As I'm writing this book, our country is on lockdown from the COVID-19 pandemic. It's a weird time. Just before the world started to close, my seventeen-year-old son, Trevor, and I were in Fort Worth, Texas, for a speaking event. I was scheduled to talk to homeschooling parents of differently wired kids about anxiety, executive functioning skills, and building a thriving homeschool experience for kids who don't fit "inside the box." Trevor was there to work in my booth and to keep me company; we love traveling together, and I try to bring one of my kids with me each time I leave for a speaking engagement.

Trevor has followed a very eclectic homeschooling model, and he's launched a pretty successful audio- and video-editing freelance business, so college after his senior year hadn't been in his plans. Instead, he'd planned to focus on growing his freelance business and possibly get another side job to get out and see other people on a regular basis because he lives with a freelancer (me) and sees that it is easy to get caught up in projects and the online world and not venture out often enough. While at the convention, though, he spent his breaks hanging out with a representative for an online college program, who talked tech with him.

Over the past weeks, my often-anxious, deep-thinking teen contemplated his past, present, and future. One night, hours after the rest of the family went to sleep, he crept downstairs from his third-floor bedroom to my first-floor office, where I was writing this manuscript. "Mom," he said, "I've been thinking. It's actually all I've been doing as I wait for audio and video to convert or render between assignments. I haven't tried very hard lately, and have been thinking that I'd like to double up my senior year next year and start taking courses with the college representative I was talking to in Texas. I could get a computer engineering degree while still growing my freelance business. I just don't think I've done enough to give myself options."

Through his deep thinking and the mindfulness strategies, he'd been using to calm his anxiety during the stress of a pandemic, and by allowing himself to really take stock of who he is and where he's going, he decided he needed something more and was ready to challenge himself to achieve new things. Since that conversation, we've connected with that representative who remembered Trevor, and he's been offered an internship with the college's tech department to help develop marketing videos and virtual reality experiences for the other students. He'll essentially be working for his degree in computer science while honing his coding and development skills in a real-world setting, all while continuing to grow his already-thriving freelance business on the side.

When we treat our sons with respect and caring and make sure they're around others who do the same, the best in them comes out. Yet, too often, we pour all our energy and time into others–the neighbors, our colleagues at work, the other parents in the district PTA, or our homeschool co-op classes–and treat our own families, and ourselves, as less. We treat others fairly and kindly and see their pain and suffering, while being overly tough, critical, doubting, suspicious, and harsh with those we love most–our children. It's a natural habit to fall into, really. We are more guarded when we're out and around others, so the ones we love most, and should be saving our best for, actually get the worst of us.

Imagine treating your son the way you would your best friend. You'd be encouraging, warm, empathetic, and there to help him heal and grow. You'd call him up (if he were a teen and a floor above you) or sit with him on the deck as the sun sets, and ask him to tell you all about his day. You'd make extra time for him. You'd pick up his favorite treats just to make him smile. Think about how your son would feel. He'd be more confident, sure of his worth, and open to loving and accepting himself. He'd be ready to hear someone like that college representative tell him that he has value and could easily pursue a degree in a field he'd only toyed with pursuing.

The more influence we have over someone, the more responsibility we have to treat them well. Think about it. Surgeons have power over their patients, and with that comes a deep-seated responsibility to care for and nurture their safety. We have so much influence over our sons, mama, that it's important to keep that in the forefront of our minds and be careful with how we treat them. If you think about your sons as people to shower with kindness and spoil with love and care, how would that change the tone you use to talk to them and the attention you take in choosing your words? If you knew they were taking in all you said and did toward them every single moment, how would that change your reactions to things like spills, meltdowns, and blowups?

They are. Your sons are watching you all the time and taking in how you talk to them and everyone else in the household. I'm not always good at remembering that and holding my tongue when I'm upset, but when I remember to think about my role as a parent like a surgeon responsible for keeping my patient alive, I do better in working to breathe life into my kids. You can do it too! I have faith in you.

Embracing the Adventure

It might sound trite, but life really is a journey. Along the road we travel with our sons, we need to help them find the tools they need to grow well. If we can teach them–and ourselves–to enjoy the adventure, we will all be much happier and more resilient. Enjoyable actions like petting the dog, chasing chickens in the yard, swimming on a hot day, or seeing friends lower stress hormones, strengthen the immune system, and help you settle when you're frustrated or worried.

As the positive feelings that result from those activities increase, so does the release of dopamine, norepinephrine, and natural opioids like endorphins–the feel-good hormones. When you want to be more motivated to do something, it's best to focus on what you love about those actions. This spurs you on and makes it easier to make time for them. Those hormones help you stay more alert and engaged, and they calm your stress and reduce emotional and physical pain.

Enjoying your life is a powerful way to take care of yourself so you can take better care of those beautiful children of yours. Think about some of the things you enjoy. For me, that includes hot coffee with fresh cream in the morning after sleeping in, a good book, snuggling on the couch with my puppy or a kiddo, and walking in the woods. What's on your list? What's on your sons' lists? Try doing this exercise yourself, then asking your sons to do it too. Compare the results and practice cultivating a family culture where you seek to do something from every member's "happy list" every single day to makes sure that everyone has a chance to find enjoyment in every day. In fact, why not make this a regular end of the day ritual? Get a journal for each of your kids and for yourself, then make time each evening to write down something that brought you joy that day (similar to the idea of a gratitude journal)–even if the joyous feeling was fleeting. It counts.

When you go out of your way to be in tune with your boys, you begin to see what they, as individuals, need to feel safe, secure, and well loved. Kids are born with a natural resilience. Think about what happens when a baby tries to roll over and gets stuck on his side, not able to make that final push over? He cries in some cases, in others he keeps rocking back and forth until he's finally propelled over. Even if he's one of those kiddos who cries first, he'll eventually try again, and again, until he finally succeeds. Resilience starts at the beginning. It's our job as mamas to help our sons become *more* resilient–to capitalize on that natural tendency and grow it.

It's stressful to be young. Our boys are rushed from lesson to lesson, activity to activity, and there's a load of pressure on them from a young age. Schedules are jam-packed, teachers and parents push hard, coaches demand stronger performance on the field, and friends encourage each other to take big risks. If that wasn't hard enough to deal with, our sons are constantly bombarded by the media and instant access to social media platforms.

Parents need to help their sons tap into their unique strengths, learn the skills to cope with these pressures, recover when things don't go their way, and be ready to tackle new challenges. Our sons cannot do this on their own.

Throughout this book, I'll share strategies for helping your boys develop the skills they need to be strong, confident, and emotionally intelligent. While the subject of this book is resiliency, much of what we'll cover is smart parenting. Listen, mama, there's no magic bullet that will instantly infuse your kiddo with all the strength he'll need to succeed. It takes calm and consistent common-sense parenting that builds on your son's natural strengths.

I want to mention briefly some tenets to this resilience-building parenting. We'll explore each more deeply throughout the book.

- ▶ Boys need absolute love and security.

- ▶ They need a deep connection with at least one adult.

- ▶ Getting out of the way can be the best thing we do for our sons.

- ▶ Listening to our sons is more important than talking to them–always.

- ▶ We should lead by example.

- ▶ Competence leads to confidence, and fostering this helps our boys move forward.

- ▶ Our sons need to understand that they control what happens to them.

- ▶ Boys with a toolbox of strategies to draw from when they feel stress will cope well with adversity.

Here's the thing, you're the absolute best mama for your sons already, so this book and the ideas and tips in here are in place to reinforce what you're already doing, validate your own right instincts, and help you get on the same page as your partner. Over the last decade, as I've written for and spoken to thousands of parents around the world, I've become known as an "expert" when it comes to parenting and homeschooling the quirkiest of kiddos. But I want you to remember this most important thing: never, ever trust any expert (even me) more than you trust your own instincts about what is right for you, your kids, and your family. YOU are the absolute best authority on your own unique sons.

I'm here to help you trust *yourself*.

Together we can grow amazing and resilient sons who are also emotional intelligent and strong.

Takeaways

▶ Mental capabilities like determination, grit, motivation, drive, self-worth, kindness, and confidence are what make your sons resilient.

▶ Resilient people see opportunities instead of setbacks.

▶ The more influence you have over someone, the more responsibility you have to treat them well.

▶ Practice cultivating a family culture where you seek to do something from every member's "happy list" every single day to makes sure that everyone has a chance to find enjoyment in every day.

▶ Resilience starts at the beginning. It's your job to help your sons become *more* resilient–to capitalize on that natural tendency and grow it.

▶ You need to help your sons tap into their unique strengths, learn the skills to cope with these pressures, recover when things don't go their way, and be ready to tackle new challenges.

▶ Never trust any expert more than you trust your own instincts about what is right for you, your kids, and your family.

Chapter Two

Emotional Intelligence

Too often we underestimate the power of a touch, a smile, a kind word, a listening ear, an honest compliment, or the smallest act of caring, all of this have the potential to turn a life around.

—Leo Buscaglia

We were having a particularly difficult year. We'd recently had a falling out with a member of our extended family and the holidays were coming, which meant that we wouldn't be seeing that person at Christmas dinner. We all needed a pick-me-up–my oldest son most of all.

Since Advent was about to start, I sat the kids down and asked what they thought of challenging ourselves to do an act of kindness every single day during all of Advent. They were excited about the idea and we began brainstorming different things we could do together to spread love in both in-person and anonymous ways. The kids came up with pages of ideas: leave dollar bills in the toy aisle at the dollar store, pay for the car behind us in a drive-through, make cards and send them to kids in the hospital, take cookies up to the police and fire stations, and so many more. We also kept a basket with candy canes, tape, bows, and little cards that read "You are important and loved...today and always, Merry Christmas" in the van in case we had a day when we hadn't reached our "kindness quota" and needed to spread some joy.

My younger kids were all over this. The girls kept little purses stuffed with those candy canes and notes to give to people wherever we went, but my son was a little more resistant. It was strange to see him act so shy, as he's kind of the most extroverted extrovert I've ever met. But with this, well, he hung back and watched.

We were in Walmart one afternoon, and it was packed. People were not showing much holiday spirit, and I just wanted to get out of there and go home with the kids. When it was our turn at checkout, I tried to smile at and make conversation with the cashier like I always do, but she was not having any of it. Her name tag read "Sonia," and she looked old and worn, with deep creases dug into her forehead, around her eyes, and on her hands. She scowled at the floor, barely looking up at me. The woman emanated negativity and sadness, and I felt my own optimism fade. I wanted to get away as quickly as possible because I was beginning to feel her hardness. She grumbled, and I felt rebuked for having had the nerve to talk to her and shrunk back, grabbing my wallet from my purse as I whispered to the kids to help put bags in the cart quickly. They were quiet, contemplative, and listened. They could feel that energy too.

Trevor watched her quietly, his eyes wide, and passed bag after bag into the cart. I breathed a sigh of relief when she handed me my receipt and we could leave. I mumbled my thanks and pushed my cart forward with the kids walking alongside me when Trevor said, "Wait, Mom."

He reached into his sister's bag, pulled out a candy cane with one of the cards taped to it, and ran back toward the cashier. He tapped her shoulder, and when she turned gruffly, he thrust the candy cane at her and whipped around, speed-walking back toward me when she took it. I was watching her. She looked bewildered for a second, then glanced at the card and back at Trevor, who had made it to me and stopped, turning back. She turned to the next customer and barked a "be right back," then shuffled over toward my son, face splitting into a smile and tears streaming. She scooped my boy up into a hug and cried while she held onto him.

When she let him go, she hugged me too and said, "Merry Christmas, beautiful family. God bless you." She then gave Trevor another quick squeeze and hurried back to her register, smiling at the customer she'd barked at a minute before.

When I asked Trevor what had prompted him to go back to her, he shrugged and said, "It just looked like she could use a smile, Mom." He made it a point from that day on to look for someone who needed a smile everywhere we went for the rest of the Advent season, producing a candy cane from his pocket each time.

Getting Involved

Emotional intelligence is the ability to manage one's own emotions as well as the emotions of others. For our sons, emotional intelligence means being able to control their own impulses, delay gratification, accept when things don't go their way, understand where others are coming from, motivate themselves, read social cues, and show compassion–both to themselves and others.

Since 1995, when Daniel Goleman's groundbreaking work on emotional intelligence (EQ) was first released, parents, teachers, doctors, therapists, scientists, and even business leaders have realized how important a role emotions play into every aspect of our lives and the lives of our children. Even more than IQ, our sons' emotional stability and strategies for dealing with feelings play a huge role in determining their success and happiness in all facets of life, including relationships and academics.

For us boy moms, this means being aware of our sons' feelings and emotions, and being able to validate, empathize with, soothe, and guide them whenever they are struggling. It also means celebrating successes and enjoying the ups with them. Too often we get caught up in the parenting and only focus on the correction, forgetting to forge the connection and celebrate both small and big accomplishments with our boys.

Goleman writes in *Emotional Intelligence: Why It Can Matter More Than IQ*, "Family life is our first school for emotional learning. In this intimate cauldron we learn how to feel about ourselves and how others will react to our feelings; how to think about these feelings and what choices we have in reacting; how to read and express hopes and fears. This emotional schooling operates not just through the things parents say and do directly to children, but also in the models they offer for handling their own feelings and those that pass between husband and wife." So how do we guide our sons–young and old–through the world of emotions? *We get involved.*

It's our job as moms to get deeply involved in the thoughts, feelings, and actions of our kiddos. I don't mean that we should micromanage them or become helicopter parents, shielding them from every little inconvenience. I *do* mean that we need to take the time to parent them through their feelings and help them name what they're experiencing, coaching them through reactions. It's easy to fall into the habit of dismissing or criticizing our sons' big feelings while we're busy doing all the things that go along with parenting.

I know that I fall into that trap from time to time. When my youngest guy doesn't want to put away his toys or video games to go to our homeschool co-op, for example, I often have a meltdown with him, barking at the kids to get in the car so we're not late. I might tell him he's being ridiculous and argumentative on purpose and that he's holding us up, sometimes bribing him to just get in the car already and letting him take his Kindle Fire with him on the drive (dismissive). Or, I might yell at him and shout that I'm sick and tired of going through this bratty behavior every single week for something *he* wants to do in the first place when I'd rather just stay home in my pajamas and read a book (criticizing).

Sometimes I even have the best intentions, and I tell him that I understand he's frustrated because he wants to play, but we do have to get going so he needs to let it go and get in the car. But, this last scenario, while being a much better option, falls a little short as well. If we truly want to teach our sons emotional intelligence, we need to mentor them through using those skills in all situations well.

In this case, the best thing I could do for Isaac would be to get down on his level, look him in the eyes, and empathize with him. I could say, "I'll bet you're frustrated because we had a busy weekend and you didn't get much time to play with the toys you love so much. I'm tired too, buddy, and I'd much rather not have to leave the house every Monday morning. But this is the day the co-op all of our friends belong to meets. We made a commitment to Miss Erin, and she is counting on us to be there." Then, I could give him a hug, squeezing so he has a chance to relax into me and let some of his tension go, and ask him what he'd most like to do as soon as we get home. Next, I could grab his hand and walk with him to the car where his siblings are waiting, listening to his plans, and we would be on our way.

It takes an extra minute or two to mentor your kiddos through tough situations, but it will become more natural as you practice getting them through their emotional responses. When you follow this type of mentoring, you acknowledge your sons' feelings, help them name them, allow them to experience those feelings, validate them, and stay with them during the moment, helping them to feel safe and heard. You don't try to dismiss the feelings or distract him from them. You help them see that feelings are normal and they're not wrong for experiencing them. You also take the extra minute or two to help them through the moment, but don't let them off the hook. Teach them that you have a responsibility to follow through on promises and commitments–in this example, the homeschool co-op we needed to get to.

You can mentor your kiddo through any tough feelings by following these steps every time:

▶ Recognize the emotion.

▶ Listen with empathy.

▶ Validate your sons.

▶ Help them label the emotion.

▶ Explore strategies to solve the problem.

Goleman and others who have studied emotional intelligence in children have noted that those who have experience being mentored through these steps and have been nurtured in this way score consistently higher academically than those whose parents followed a more dismissive or criticizing approach. They get along better with peers and other adults in their lives, and they have fewer behavioral problems. They've also noted that adults who have a strong emotional intelligence are more successful in their careers and in their relationships. Children and adults with stronger emotional intelligence experience fewer negative feelings and more positive ones, and they are more well-rounded overall.

What's even more important, children who have stronger emotional intelligence and who come from homes where they are regularly mentored in this way show more confidence and resilience. They still get sad, angry, frustrated, or scared, but they are better able to bounce back from these setbacks.

An important thing for us to remember here, mama, is that adopting this approach to parenting boys through their emotions, while guaranteed to build stronger sons, won't eliminate conflict altogether. It is, however, a much healthier response to conflict. We're honoring and validating our sons' emotions, which is the opposite of encouraging them to "suck it up" or "be a man." Mentoring your sons through their emotional reactions builds connections and deepens the sense of *team* that brings families together.

Family arguments, sibling rivalry, and the need for discipline are part of living life together as a family. I will say, though, that the strategies in this chapter and later in this book will bring you closer to your sons. And, when your family shares a deeper bond and mutual respect, problems seem lighter and are easier to deal with.

Discipline, too, becomes easier. When you and your children are emotionally connected in this way, you're more invested in their lives and your words matter more to them than ever before. You all truly know and trust that you're in this life together, living side by side through it. You can be tough and call your kiddos on their behavior when you see them making choices that can be detrimental to their future. They'll listen more because they know, from your conversations and support, that you have their best interests in mind. This tends to motivate them more to change their course or not make those negative choices in the first place.

Mentoring Your Boy

Have you ever laughed at your teeny toddler or preschooler when he's stomped off in a huff after something didn't go his way? It can be quite funny to see this little person spewing huge feelings all over the place, and the instinct to laugh comes bubbling out. But imagine if you laughed when your husband had a bad day and was venting to you about it when he got home from work. Or if your best friend was struggling and came to you for support; imagine laughing at her. It probably wouldn't go well in either of those situations and could permanently damage the trust in both of those relationships. But so many of us don't even think twice about laughing at our kids when they're experiencing big feelings.

If your spouse woke up in a cold sweat from a nightmare, you'd let him talk it through and comfort him. But when your son–who rarely sleeps through the night–has another bad dream, you dismiss him, telling him to go back to bed because there is nothing to be afraid of (and you just want to sleep).

Remember that a key step in helping your sons develop emotional intelligence is to empathize with them and validate their feelings. You need to do this even when it's in the middle of the night or when they look really cute and funny and we just want to burst out laughing. You need to do this even when you're talking to a friend or our spouse or when you are running late to be somewhere. If you're constantly invalidating what your sons are feeling, you send them the subtle message that they shouldn't trust their own feelings, and their confidence plummets.

I know that, when it's time to launch my sons out into the world, I want them to be able to trust their feelings and emotions, stand up for what is right, nurture those around them, and bring strength and happiness to whomever they love. I want them to weather the storms that are tossed their way. I don't want them to fall prey to the societal belief that children are less than adults just because they're smaller and lack rationality. And I don't want us to fall into that belief system either, mama. Our sons may be less experienced, but their thoughts, feelings, emotions, and plans are just as important and valid as ours.

Taking their emotions as seriously as they are meant to be taken requires empathetic listening skills and the willingness (and ability) to see things from their perspective. It also takes a special kind of selflessness because they typically want us to solve their problems immediately. In fact, behavioral psychologists have estimated that preschoolers typically demand their parents attend to their needs or desires at an average rate of three times per minute. I don't know if that's actually true, but it certainly feels like it most days. And it doesn't end when the preschool days give way to the elementary or intermediate years. Young tweens and teens are just as needy in different ways.

I have a seven-year-old son who needs me throughout the day. He is an early riser and I'm not, and he loves cuddling and telling me about the plans he has for the day each morning as I force my eyes open and caffeinate. I hear about his dreams–good and bad–and the things he wants to do once he's finished with his school work for the day. Once his sister gets up, he goes off with her to get some cereal and I finish gulping my coffee to clear the cobwebs, but from that moment on, I'm on call to attend to, validate, and empathize with my kids all day long.

As I work from home and homeschool my four kids, I tend to work late into the night. It's usually calm and quiet as the littler two children settle in for sleep, my husband goes to bed, and my teen daughter goes online to connect with some of her friends over some video game or another. As the house settles and quiets, though, my teen son emerges and makes frequent stops in or around my office. Eventually, he pops over the gate I have in the doorway to keep the dog out since I don't have a door and plops himself down on a nearby armchair. And he talks. And talks. And talks.

Talking to your teens takes a different kind of mentoring than soothing young boys when they don't want to go somewhere or "aren't sleepy." It's more important now than ever before to be available to help them through their big thoughts whenever they're ready to talk about things. Now, when my son settles down and lets out a sigh, I get ready to validate his feelings and talk him through anxious thoughts about growing up, getting a degree, growing his business, moving out...all the things that are big and scary about becoming an adult. And being there pays off. As I'm writing this chapter, my son just popped into my office and told me I was pretty. An unsolicited compliment, without him wanting something from it, was such a nice surprise while I've been sweating over this keyboard (literally, as it's 90 degrees and our air conditioner isn't working). Being a boy mom is so wonderful sometimes.

If we want our boys to grow into men of character, resilience, and confident maturity, and to become fathers who love and support their families, truly empathizing with their wives and children, then we need to model those characteristics and reinforce them now. Moms of boys should show genuine respect for their sons' feelings from the time they're infants through young adulthood and beyond. They must empathize and communicate in a way that preserves both their own self-respect and that of their sons. Understanding, connection, and empathy should always come before correction and advice. I like to remind myself, and my husband, to *connect before we correct*.

It's important not to tell our sons what they should feel in certain situations because it makes our boys begin to doubt themselves, and as we'll explore later in this book, it's critical that our sons know they have control over the way their life is lived. Boys' emotions don't disappear when their mom tells them not to feel badly or that something isn't as scary as they're making it out to be. All feelings are just and valid. I tell my own kids and the kids I work with that all feelings are valid, but not all behavior is acceptable. I teach them that they absolutely have control over the way they behave in reaction to things, that they are allowed to feel whatever they do, but they should watch how they react. It's okay for us mamas to set boundaries when it comes to actions and reactions, but it's not okay to limit feelings, emotions, and desires.

Takeaways

▶ Emotional stability plays a huge role in determining your sons' success and happiness in life.

▶ Practice mentoring your sons through their emotional responses so it becomes natural to you.

▶ Boys with strong emotional intelligence still feel sad, scared, frustrated, and other negative emotions, they just bounce back from them more quickly than others.

▶ When you and your sons are emotionally connected, your words matter more to him than ever before.

▶ The key step to helping your sons develop emotional intelligence is to empathize with them and validate their feelings.

▶ Connect before you correct.

Chapter Three

Strong Mothering

Family is not an important thing;
it is everything.

—Michael J. Fox

"I have a video to show you. Remind me when we're alone," my friend Erin said to me one day when we met up at our local homeschool field trip group's weekly get-together. Her family is one of my kids' absolute favorites, and we're so blessed that they're homeschooling alongside us. There's a kid for each of my kids–boy, girl, girl, boy–in the same order and close to the same ages. Friends have come and gone in co-ops and play groups and other homeschool social meetups, but if Erin's family is going to be where we're going, my kids are always on board.

There's a sort of synchronicity our kids feel when they're together. Part of the reason is we're both raising kids with a variety of differently wired brains. Giftedness, dyslexia, anxiety disorder, sensory issues, and emotional overexcitabilities are all "challenges" that are sprinkled throughout both families. The kids just *get* each other. And, as Erin and I are both parenting similarly wired kiddos, we share some of the same unique challenges. So, when she said that to me but wasn't offering up the chance to see this video to the other moms in the group, I knew it would be something I could relate to.

We were at a park that day, and it was an exercise in herding cats to make sure the little kids didn't wander off, stayed where we could see them, and weren't plummeting to their deaths on the playground's zip line. It was an exhausting day, full of laughs and fun, but Erin and I didn't have time to slip away, so once we got all our kids in the vans and settled with snacks, she pulled her phone out to show me a video of her youngest, Griffin.

Griffin was just under two at the time, and hilarious. My kids joked that he must be part of a secret underground spy ring that hid agents in plain sight as little kids with big eyes and serious souls. Griffin was an old man in a teeny tiny body. If you looked deeply into his eyes, you would swear that you could see history. He was quiet, contemplative, sweet, and a complete mama's boy. He hung the sun, moon, and stars on Erin and never let her out of his sight. And he was so smart and intuitive, which furthered my kids' suspicions that he was actually super-secret-spy-kid Griffin.

In the video, Griffin was wide eyed, tears brimming and spilling over the edge of his gorgeous lashes. He looked devastated. Hair disheveled from playing happily moments before, his face was crumbled and trembling. As the video clip ended, he reached off frame and wept in his mother's arms. It was the saddest and sweetest thing I had ever seen. What triggered this emotional outpouring in this teeny tiny tot? His mama had played the song "You Are My Sunshine," and it broke him.

Griffin shows a highly sensitive nature and emotional overexcitabilities. These characteristics make him more in tune to the feelings of people around him and give him the ability to pick up nonverbal cues well. Highly sensitive kiddos are wonderful, and so tiring. They feel high highs and low lows, and they tend to be most attached to whichever parent understands them the most. In this case, it's his mama. His mom does a wonderful job tuning in to all of her children's needs and feelings. She talks them through things and tries to understand their perspective before offering them advice.

Nurturing Your Own Emotional Intelligence

In order to nurture sensitivity and other emotional intelligence traits in our sons like Erin does, whether our boys come by it naturally or not, we need to be in tune with our *own* emotional intelligence. All emotions–sadness, anger, fear, stress, and so on–can be useful, so we need to know what we're feeling and how we react to those feelings in order to mentor our sons through them as they come up in their lives. Anger can move us forward to fight injustices by learning about the government and protesting peacefully. Stress can cause a buildup of energy that we can channel to tackle all those home improvement projects we've wanted to get started on.

When my oldest son was little, we talked about getting chickens for our backyard, but we couldn't have them in the neighborhood we were living in at the time. Fast-forward to March 2020 when our country was suddenly shut down due to a pandemic, and my husband–a first-grade reading specialist–was thrown into the world of online teaching and was under tremendous stress due to learning new technologies and methodologies, other administrative aspects of his job, and migrating to working from home within a household where the rest of the family was set in our ways. I work from home as an educational coach, consultant, author, speaker, blogger, and podcaster, and I've homeschooled our four kids since the oldest was in first grade. He is now seventeen. It's safe to say that we have our own kind of rhythm to our day, one that is not in tune with my husband's natural rhythms.

One day, when my husband went out to get groceries, he came home with a dozen chicks from the Tractor Supply across the parking lot from the grocer because "he might as well try to raise them now that he's home and we're living somewhere we can have them."

Two of my kids are very much like my husband; stress brings out the tinkering gene, and they work on projects, so this has been a great activity for the three of them. They've built coops, tracked down runaway hens, and trained our pug to herd them away from the road (for real!). When we can teach our kids that all emotions can be used and channeled for good and model that for them, we mentor them toward a healthy relationship with their emotions.

When I'm feeling depressed, I know it's time for me to see where I'm overspent and pay attention to the positives in my life. I then work on letting go of the stuff that is overwhelming me and focus more on the good. I try to mentor my oldest to do this too. Trevor is prone to anxiety, and over the years we've developed whole toolboxes of strategies (tips, tricks, activities, scripts, fidgets, etc.) to help break him and his sister, who also struggles with generalized anxiety disorder, of the negative thought loops. Instead of telling him it's going to be fine or that what he's worried about isn't likely to happen, I try to use his vulnerability and openness to build our relationship. I can let him talk and let out what's weighing on him, and coach him through those thoughts.

If he's having trouble putting a name to his feelings, I can be there to help him identify what's going on. It's brought us closer through the years, and I really enjoy our conversations. I love that he comes to me to process the things that are swirling around in his mind. When we can take the time to see inside our kiddos' minds and emotions, we're better able to be patient with them when they're sad, angry, or afraid. We're more willing to sit with our crying preschooler or listen to our tween's venting.

My friend Jen says that when she takes the time to listen to her son's point of view, it makes him feel better because they are resolving issues on terms he has a stake in. It's like a win-win. They're settling their differences like two equal human beings, not like a ruler and her subject. She goes on to say that when her boys argue, she encourages them to be honest but not hurtful with one another. "It's important they be able to communicate their anger in constructive ways, and for them to know that being angry isn't bad and that it doesn't mean they hate each other. It's just a normal part of living with others. I tell them that they can be mad at their brothers, but family is their safety net and the people they can always turn to when they need support, so they don't want to push each other away."

Teaching your boys that you accept all feelings, but not all behaviors is a key to good mentoring. They know that you'll step in if their behaviors are harmful to themselves or others, but they also know that you're not going to shield them from emotionally charged situations because they need to learn to regulate their emotions. This isn't always easy, though. It's tough to watch your kids navigate disappointment and grapple with adversity. Remember, though, when you mentor your sons through their frustration now, they'll be better equipped to cope with bigger disappointments later on in life when they need to.

Their resiliency grows with them.

By mentoring your sons' through these feelings now, they'll know how to react when facing disappointment ten years from now, and they'll know there are proactive things they can do to help themselves deal with that frustration in a socially acceptable way.

The best parent mentors for their children are also not afraid to show their own emotions to their sons. Your kids should see you cry when you're sad, mama. It's okay to yell when you're frustrated or angry, again, talking through feelings with your sons. When they see you lose your temper, regroup, talk about it, and ask for forgiveness. They will learn to do the same. It's unreasonable to expect that they'll never yell (or that you won't). When you model the best way to react and seek forgiveness, it is a gift that will serve them in their relationships for their whole life.

When you're an emotional mentor to your kiddos and you say or do something that is hurtful (which happens all the time in families–you're not alone), don't be afraid to apologize. Under stress you act without thinking. We all do. Regretting those actions is maturity and when you tell your sons you're sorry and how you were feeling in that moment, you have the opportunity to tell them how you think you should have handled it, and how you'll do better next time. You're showing your sons how to deal with difficult feelings and be better able to deal with their own in the future.

The amazing thing about adopting this kind of mentoring approach to parenting for emotional intelligence is that family conflict actually lessens so you spend more time enjoying one another's company and less time falling into disciplinary issues. There are several reasons for this.

One, when kids are mentored through their emotions from a young age, they learn early on the art of self-soothing. They can stay calm under stress and process difficult emotions, giving them less reason to misbehave.

Two, since mothers who mentor their sons through their emotions consistently respond to their sons before their emotions escalate, their boys don't have to ramp things up to get the attention they need and want. Over time, boys gain a clear understanding of how much their moms understand, empathize, and care for them. They feel safe and don't have to act out to test their security.

And three, there are fewer opportunities for conflict between moms and their sons when their boys know that their feelings won't be disapproved of. Remember, when you're mentoring your sons through their emotional challenges, you're focused on their behaviors and reactions, and you're not reprimanding them because they're angry, sad, or are crying.

Finally, this style of parenting strengthens the emotional bond between parent and child so that sons are more responsive to their mothers' requests. These boys see their moms as their confidantes and allies and want to please them. They don't want to be a disappointment.

Begin with Yourself

There's a reason we're instructed to secure our own oxygen mask first when we're on an airplane and the flight attendant is going through the safety information. In a very practical sense, if mom passes out from lack of oxygen, she can't help anyone. So we're told that the first thing we need to do in an emergency is to take care of ourselves, make sure the oxygen is flowing well, then turn to each of our kiddos to help them adjust their own masks. Once we're taken care of, we'll have the strength to take care of our children in any situation.

It's the same with mentoring your sons through their emotional regulation. It's really difficult to be a great mother when you've allowed yourself to become depleted, frustrated, and out of touch with your own emotional needs. And moms tend to be the one in the family that their sons go to for everything emotional.

Are you your sons' *person*? Meaning, do your sons come to you for anything and everything? It can be exhausting and amazing all at the same time to be your kiddos' person, but it's when we're overwhelmed with our own and others' emotions, and we're frustrated with the lack of time we have to do and be all the things to everyone, that we start doubting ourselves and our worth as mothers. And we're no good to anyone at that point.

Not taking care of your emotions can lead to poor health and increased stress, anxiety, and even mental health issues. The following sections will cover strategies to help you address your own emotional needs.

Share Your Feelings

We know that how we talk to our sons about their feelings can influence their social, emotional, and academic well-being, but we forget that in order to successfully mentor our boys through their emotions we have to be in control of our own.

Remember that actions speak louder than words, so be really cognizant of how you react to emotional stress. When you're feeling anxious, talk about it with your kids. Share with them what you're feeling and experiencing.

I've been a public speaker for years. I was on the speech and debate team in college and have spoken at workshops, conferences, and conventions in a variety of subject areas, from teaching and writing to parenting and more. I get paid to speak at events, and my kids know that it's an important part of my job and a major reason that I am able to stay home with them and homeschool. But I still get nervous, especially when I'm debuting a new talk or speaking on a new topic. And I talk to my kids about that.

I might say to my teen when he travels with me, "I'm feeling a little sick to my stomach right now. My nerves are bubbling up inside of me. Have you ever felt that way? That palpable roiling, clawing feeling just before you are about to do something new and a little scary? I'm feeling that way right now. I'm about to go talk to several hundred parents about helping their kiddos with anxiety and here I am feeling my own anxiety taking me down. I have to go to the ballroom right now and get set up, but I'd love a hug from you and for you to say a prayer for me while I'm speaking if you don't mind."

Sharing our feelings, struggles, and stressors with our sons and asking them to help in whatever way makes the most sense for you can be an amazing gift to them. It shows them that you have the same emotions they feel from time to time, helps them put words to their feelings, shows them some strategies for working through them, and then puts them on your team by asking them to help you through your challenges. They'll be more likely to do the same the next time they're feeling stressed or overwhelmed.

Ask for Help

It's important to listen to your mind and body when it comes to regulating your own emotions. We often forget that it's crucial to our mental well-being to say *no* to things that make us uncomfortable whenever possible. For example, calling people on the phone causes me anxiety. I'm not proud of that, but I do know that I'm much better in writing (text and email) than I am on the phone. I tend to ramble and talk in circles, filling the pauses nervously. Sure, I can talk on the phone when I need to. I spent an hour and a half on the phone just the other day, talking to a potential client about some marketing work I think would be beneficial for his company as well as the parents I serve through my website and podcasts. I put off that call for several days, though. Not for any reason other than I much prefer to have the time to think through my words carefully, and writing gives me a better chance to do that.

Because of this anxiety, my husband makes most of the phone calls related to anything that goes wrong or right in our lives. He's the one who calls credit card companies to dispute fraudulent charges (and I sit next to him so I can take the phone periodically to confirm that, yes, I do give him permission to take care of this on my behalf). I avoid situations that spike my anxiety when I can. This allows me to store up the reserves I need to handle the situations I can't avoid with calm emotions and grace. My sons see my husband doing things like this for me. More importantly, though, they see me *asking* him to do those things for me.

Asking for help when you know you'll be emotionally dysregulated shows maturity and confidence. I want my boys to be confident and mature enough to ask for help on the things that really stretch them emotionally. It might not always be possible to avoid the situation or activity, or to allow them to do so, but by taking care of your needs in this way, you're showing them how to care for themselves and others. You're

Raising Resilient Sons

also preserving your own energy for the things you can handle and knowing your own limits.

Invite Joy

Just as important as avoiding some of those things that trigger negative emotions, though, is to seek out things that bring you joy. The absolute best way to develop and nurture your own resiliency is to bring joy into your life. Choose to take a day off and read a great book. Make a new habit of taking your first cup of coffee each morning out to the yard or onto your deck and sit with it, soaking up the sun and birdsongs. Choose a show to watch with your kids each week or a new series to binge with them on Netflix. My daughter and I tuned into *American Idol* every week during its historic "at-home pandemic" season, while my teen son and I chose to unwind by watching an episode of *Sherlock*, *Doctor Who*, or *Merlin* each night.

Taking time for things that bring you joy will help you have the energy to regulate your emotions when things go wrong–and they will. You are part of a family with all the quirks that go along with multiple people living in close quarters with one another, and if you're not finding joy in something every single day, you're going to struggle emotionally. That will be a tough burden for you to bear, and you won't have anything left over to be able to use in your role as an emotional mentor to your sons.

Takeaways

▶ In order to nurture sensitivity and other emotional intelligence traits in your sons, you need to be in tune with your own emotional intelligence.

▶ When you can teach your kids that all emotions can be used and channeled for good, you help foster healthy reactions toward emotions.

▶ Teaching boys that all feelings are acceptable, but behaviors need to be controlled and monitored, is crucial while growing resiliency.

▶ Adopting a mentoring approach to parenting through emotions reduces the amount of time you spend in conflict with your sons, strengthening your family's bond.

▶ Be aware of your own emotional regulation and put on your oxygen mask first when you need it.

▶ Controlling and regulating your emotions, and stepping away or finding joy when you need to, are powerful demonstrations of maturity and strength your kids *will* see.

Part Two

Letting Go

*It's time to add a pinch of adventure,
a sprinkle of green time, and
a big handful of play.*

—Penny Whitehouse

When I think of little boys, I see images of denim overalls and ripped knees, muddy faces, and frogs in pockets. Those iconic pictures of fishing and biking and rocket-making flash before me. Moms of boys know what it's like to go for a walk and see our little ones pick up sticks to brandish as swords, protecting us from imaginary danger. Our small heroes are there for us. We also know what it's like to see them grab something that moved suddenly and to say a silent, quick prayer that it wasn't something venomous.

Little boys dig holes, jump on couch cushions they've taken off and piled high on the floor, and chase puppies around the yard endlessly until they all fall into a heap, panting together. Bigger boys experiment with Diet Coke and Mentos explosions, rocket launches, and making slingshots out of V-shaped branches. Even bigger boys wrestle with their friends, shoot water bottles with pellet guns, and set up servers for their favorite video games so they can play together anytime their friends are available.

Girls do some of these things too, while many boys are calmer and more easily content than their more boisterous counterparts, but we seem to be caught in this loop of forgetting, as a society, that girls and boys *can* (and do) bring different gifts into the world. We need to let boyhood stand, allow our boys to be boys–in whatever way that means to *our individual* boys– and guide those precious gifts toward helping them grow into kind, confident, and emotionally strong men.

We *can* do this, mamas. But we need to let go of the pressure to conform to society. It's time to forget about what the other moms say we should be doing and follow our own instincts. We are perfect for our sons, and they are perfect for us. Let's remember that the next time we have the instinct to push or correct, rather than to connect.

For example, how often have you watched a friend's son dominate on the basketball court, then put pressure on your own son to practice more, try harder, *be* better? Or when was the last time you worried so much you started pricing tutors because your cousin's son was two grade levels ahead in math and your son was struggling with his current grade level?

It's natural to worry and to wonder if we are doing what's best for our sons, but the pushing that often goes along with that concern is where we get ourselves into trouble.

The better option is to let go of the need to control outcomes. Be there for your sons. Ask them what they think about the game they just played or the test they just took, and why. Take a look at the things your sons are involved in, which of those they're truly interested in, and what can be trimmed. Become a student of your sons so you can capitalize on their interests and help them grow in ways that feed into their natural gifts. They are who they're meant to be, your job is to help them grow in those gifts.

Letting go of your own expectations for what your boys' childhood should include as well as the pressure to go along with the overscheduled crowd can yield big results, build relationships with your boys, and empower them to trust their own dreams and desires.

It can make you happier too.

Chapter Four

At Play

Play builds the kind of free-and-easy, try-it-out, do-it-yourself character that our future needs.

— James L. Hymes, Jr.

I watched from the kitchen window as my son Trevor climbed higher and higher in the tree just across the yard. His friend gazed up at him from below, shouting that he was going too high. I was uneasy; I had a feeling that this wouldn't end well, but I knew he needed to be brave and push his limits, so I watched while aimlessly moving the dishes around the sink instead of washing them.

Trevor's smile lit up the yard, and his friend Carlos whooped from below, impressed now that he knew his friend had made it to a high lookout spot. I turned from the window and went to get a snack ready for the adventurers.

As I made my way across the yard, I heard Carlos shouting up at Trevor, "No! Your other foot! You got it! Yay! You're almost there."

I watched, heart racing, as my five-year-old boy made it back down the tree, coached by his friend. I hung back a bit, though it was *really* hard for me. Trevor dropped to the ground, high-fived his friend, and noticed me, "Mommy, I got stuck. I climbed too high and couldn't get back down, but Carlos helped me." My courageous boy looked up at me, eyes shining.

I'll never forget that moment.

"Amazing," I told him. "You both did a great job problem solving, and I bet you adventurers are hungry."

He and his buddy grabbed for the snack, chattering away about the deserted island they'd been "playing on," the plane they'd imagined they'd heard, and how Trevor had scaled the highest "palm tree" to wave it down to rescue them. That's why Carlos had whooped with joy–their efforts succeeded and the game was won. Just before Trevor had realized he was stuck, the rescue plane began its descent and they knew they'd be home with their loved ones again. Instead of panicking, his friend had guided him down by telling him where to put his feet and hands, and positioning himself beneath to catch him if he fell.

They'd solved their problems together, and I left them to snack and adventure some more.

The Power of Play

While Trevor's adventures to the top of the tree weren't problem-free, they were *his*. Adults weren't around to choose their games or tell those boys to stay out of the trees and keep their feet on the ground. The autonomy of choosing for themselves is an important characteristic of play, and play is what shapes our kids as they become the adults they're supposed to be.

Dr. Peter Gray, author of *Free to Learn*, defines play as inherently self-chosen and self-directed, intrinsically motivated, guided by self-imposed rules with room for creativity, active, and free of stress. Play is chosen by the participants for no other reason but its own sake. It spans across ages and generations. He goes on to explain that play is where kids discover their passions and develop skills related to them, learn how to get along with one another despite their disagreements, solve their own problems, get out of the predicaments they get themselves into, and control their emotions. He says that these are all crucial lessons that can't be taught in school or by other, adult-directed means; they can only be learned through free, self-directed play.

Fred Rogers once said, "Play is often talked about as if it were a relief from serious learning. But for children play is serious learning. Play really is the work of childhood." Gray agrees. In an interview on the *Raising Lifelong Learners* podcast, he told me that children from all cultures and eras play with the tools they need to make sense of the adult world they're growing into. For the hunter-gatherer cultures he studied, those tools were bows, arrows, scythes, and fire. For our kids, those tools are computers, tablets, books, art supplies, cooking ingredients and supplies, and so much more.

Play helps kids build strength, confidence, and emotional regulation. In recent years, though, play as defined by Dr. Gray, has become more and more obsolete. Recess has been cut to the bare minimum in schools across the country. Playdates are structured. Boyhood has become a time of jam-packed schedules and running from activity to activity. Children go to lessons and classes all day, then are rushed off to music, sports, theater, and other things all evening long. Then parental peer pressure kicks in, and moms schedule extra practice sessions, tutoring, new classes, and more performance opportunities. Gone are the days of packs of kids riding bikes and throwing footballs on cul-de-sacs across the country.

It's no wonder that, according to the National Institutes for Mental Health, as many as 39.1 percent of children will be diagnosed with an anxiety disorder by the time they're eighteen. When parents overschedule their children, they have less time for the child-centered play that is crucial for healthy development. Unstructured play and downtime give children the opportunity to develop passions, interests, and competencies of their own choosing and significantly lowers their stress.

Play gives boys the chance to demonstrate and build their creativity, problem-solving skills, and emotional growth. It gives our sons a chance to share, negotiate, nurture others, stand up against injustices, and advocate for themselves. These are best observed in one of the most ideal play situations: when groups of mixed-aged children are playing together. I overheard my seven-year-old saying to one of the kids on the playground during our homeschool co-op's lunch break that he was tired of always playing the games the big kids wanted to play, and it was time for the little guys to have a chance (his words). Those "big kids," the twelve-year-olds, told him he was right, they had been choosing the games, and asked Isaac what he wanted to play.

We don't have to step in and do the work for our sons. They'll step up and into their own courage when we let go and let them lead.

One of the best things about this unprecedented time we're living through as I write this book is that families all across the country have been forced to slow down, embrace family time, and plan for a day-camp-and-activity-free summer. Now, I'm not trying to downplay the hardship that this is causing for so many families with regard to childcare and lost wages and illness, but when it comes to looking at this time with a specific lens on childhood, I've enjoyed the things I've seen.

Friends in my Facebook feed have started interesting family traditions. One family has a night each week where her three sons are completely in charge of the meal preparation. They rotate who is in charge of an appetizer, main meal, and dessert each week, and they must plan it all out in advance so the ingredients get put on the grocery list. No plan is too ambitious, and these kids have tried some really interesting foods. They'd also never cooked before because they are an extremely busy family that starts their days super early with hockey practice, followed by school for the kids and work for both mom and dad, a quick dinner and homework session, then off to more activities, finally dropping exhausted into bed after a long day, only to repeat it the next day.

My kids have enjoyed a kind of throwback summer vibe. One kiddo is experimenting in the kitchen while chatting online with friends from around the country. They've come together for board games and late-night swims, and my seventeen-year-old son is teaching my seven-year-old son to play chess. Now that things are starting to open back up again, we've been getting together weekly with another family who has also been sheltering-in-place for months. All eight of our kids, used to meeting up and taking classes together at our co-op, going to the zoo, or taking a field trip, are running and playing in backyards, riding bikes, jumping on trampolines in the rain, then doing belly slides in overflowing ditches. They're licking drippy popsicles as they melt, fingers and chins stained purple. They're inventing games, solving conflict, and living life together. This slower, simpler time free of organized activity has been good for so many families I know.

Normal learning happens through play because kids are wired to discover and adapt to their environment. Consider this study from 1999. Sugata Mitra, researcher of educational technology, along with his colleagues, designed the "Hole in the Wall" experiments where they placed a computer in a kiosk in a hole in the wall in the poor areas of Delhi. They monitored the computer via hidden camera and watched as children played with the computers, eventually teaching themselves how to use the preloaded programs, access the internet, play games, and to read. The study was replicated with similar results in other parts of India and in Cambodia.

What was most striking about Mitra's studies was how the children of varying ages worked together to scaffold their new knowledge. As each child learned something new about the computers, or the world around them *from* the computers, they shared that knowledge with other kids and grew their knowledge base exponentially and collaboratively.

In *Free to Learn*, Peter Gray highlights how the three core aspects of human nature–curiosity, playfulness, and sociability–can combine to serve the purpose of education. In this case, *curiosity* draws the children in to investigate the computers, *playfulness* prompts them to practice and explore a variety of computer skills, and their drive to be *social* motivates them to spread that learning to dozens of other children in their villages.

This same set of instincts can be harnessed to build strong, confident, courageous, perseverant, resilient, and caring sons.

Getting Out of the Way

As our sons develop, learn, and grow, they increase their competence in all aspects of their lives. Think about it, tiny tots are learning to crawl, walk, then run, while our teens are learning how they fit into the adult world, with the help of our guidance. They're balancing between milestones, and how we react is the key to their motivation, success, and confidence.

While we want to celebrate each of our kiddos' milestones, sometimes we go overboard in our excitement about raising sons and overpower our boys. It's natural to want to protect our sons from hurt. In fact, I was just talking about this with a friend the other day. We were talking about our concerns for our teen boys. Her son first experienced how quickly false rumors can take hold when he, his sisters, and a few neighborhood friends were all playing together.

One of the neighborhood girls told another that he had kissed her–which wasn't true–and that girl told the other boys and then his sister, who told their mom. When my friend asked her son about the kiss, he was stunned and upset that someone would say that about him, and after talking it out, despite her instinct to call the girl's mother and confront the situation, she encouraged her son to be proactive and ask the girl to stop saying things about him that were not true, and the issue was resolved for the time being.

So many of us fall into the habit of hovering, praising, protecting, and *overprotecting* our sons, and while involved parents *do* raise motivated children, there needs to be a balance. Overly involved parents can erode their children's confidence, unintentionally reinforcing the idea that they're not in control of their own lives and that things happen *to* them, instead of them making things happen.

To help them build confidence and grow resilience, we need to get out of their way, allowing them to solve problems on their own, coming to us for counsel and help when they're up against a new situation. We also need to jump in with our sons and help them build new areas of competence and skill. Finally, we need to let them know that we're there to help them think through situations wisely and safely, and that they can come to us if they need support.

Like my friend's son, my oldest had his first uncomfortable situation with a girl recently, and we worked out a solution together. He was in a play, and one of the other teen actors, a sweet girl he enjoyed chatting with backstage, developed a crush on him. He did not feel the same way and thought she understood that. He panicked, though, when she texted him one weeknight, asking if he wanted to "hang out" sometime. He had no idea what to say to her as he'd thought he'd made it clear he wasn't interested in dating her, and that he thought of her as a friend. He stewed about it for hours, talked to his twelve-year-old sister about how he should respond to the girl's text, then ultimately came to me to ask for help in letting her down gently without hurting her feelings. He understood that if she'd been brave enough to ask him out, she'd be hurt when he told her again that he wasn't interested in anything more than friendship. He understood that this could hurt her. I told him that he needed to write back to her and be honest, and that I'd be happy to proofread his text before he sent it so he could make sure that it was kind enough to avoid hurting her. Ultimately, he knew his castmate best and needed to understand how to let someone down gently.

It's hard to get out of the way. We naturally want to fix our sons' problems and guide them to success. But, when we let them figure things out for themselves, we send a powerful message to that we believe they are able. When our little boys are out in the yard balancing large branches together to make a shelter and we watch, cheering from the deck, we send the message that they are capable. When those branches fall into a pile and they try to rebuild the stick fort without us swooping in to help, we send a new message. We show them that we respect when they try again.

Each time we jump in and solve problems for our sons, we take a little away from their growing sense of competence. We tell them by our actions that they are dependent on us. While there's a small part of a mom that wants her children to need her forever, we need to remember that our job is to raise strong, capable *adult* men.

And getting out of their way doesn't mean that we abandon them to their own devices. No, we need to support their problem-solving skills by being available to offer gentle guidance when they ask for it or when it's absolutely necessary. In this way we can foster their growing resilience and independence, and help them see their own strength.

Many parents–me included–struggle with the question of when to jump in and when to let our kids make choices on their own. In his book, *Parent Effectiveness Training*, Thomas Gordon, PhD, suggests that parents decide who owns the problem. If it is a problem that a child is facing in his own life, independent of his parents, like an issue with a friend or a conflict at school, then parents are most helpful acting as counsel and not trying to actually solve the problem for their son. They can get out of their son's way or help him by using strategies like role playing, guided questioning, or having a conversation with him.

However, if a son's problem or his behavior is interfering with his parents' or siblings' lives, then parents have the right to be a little more direct. For example, two of my kiddos are night owls like me. The bulk of this book was written between the hours of 10 p.m. and 2 a.m. for various reasons, including the fact that those same children are around and in my hair all day long while we homeschool and there are lessons to finish, meals to prepare, and games to play. When I stay up late to work, though, I'm in my office on the first floor and keep quiet.

Recently my husband and I had to sit down with our two night owls and tell them that they would either need to start heading to bed a lot earlier in the evening, be much quieter, or we'd have to talk about consequences like losing internet or phone privileges. They started retreating to their rooms after dinner, then coming back out once their younger siblings were in bed. But they were loud–really loud. It disrupted my husband, who goes to sleep early. They often woke the younger kids, who struggled to get back to sleep, and they distracted me from work. So, since their choices caused problems for other people in our household, it was time for mom and dad to step in and help them problem solve.

The challenge comes in when we fall into the cycle of solving too much for our kids. You know what I'm talking about, right? When we think we know exactly what our sons need to do in order to solve a problem or make something happen, we start by telling them what's wrong with what they're doing, and then we lecture them (endlessly) all about everything that could possibly happen negatively as a result of their behavior.

The thing to ask ourselves, moms, is why we're so caught up in the outcome. Is it because

▶ We're afraid they won't be successful?

▶ We think they are being lazy?

▶ We are embarrassed by their choices or behaviors and think it reflects poorly on us?

▶ We are perfectionistic and see our kids as reflections of ourselves?

▶ We want to shelter our sons from the pain of making mistakes?

► We mistake criticism for guidance and judge in order to facilitate our sons' improved behavior?

When we value our own solutions over our that of our sons, we send them a clear message: we don't think they can handle their own lives. But if we want our sons to grow to be resilient and emotionally strong, we can cultivate that by encouraging autonomy and experimentation.

Letting Our Kids Lead

Some children seem self-directed from the get-go. They're wide-eyed infants who take in their surroundings completely before finally crashing late at night when there's nothing else to see. They're toddlers who pull out everything from any cupboard they can reach and bang on pots and pans while you cook. They're children who create imaginary worlds complete with languages and currencies and draw all the neighborhood children into their game too. They're teens who follow a nontraditional path to their education and start their own businesses while concurrently taking high school classes, and decide that college isn't for them.

Following your son's lead can be scary. Recognizing him as an autonomous being is terrifying.

Parents often think that their child is passionate and self-driven when it comes to sports or an outside activity, and if that desire to pursue excellence in an area is truly coming from your son then it should be supported and nurtured. However, if your son's drive is motivated by the desire to please us instead of the joy of the activity, then it will eventually become a source of stress in his life. You can actively expose your sons to different options and support them, but ultimately the direction for what they stick with needs to come from them. And, sometimes, even when we think we've helped them figure out what makes them light up, we need to watch them, learn from them, and reevaluate like Gavin's parents recently did.

Fifteen-year-old Gavin has played the guitar for years. He has taken private lessons and plays for two teen rock bands. During the spring and summer months, he and his band perform at events all around Northeast Ohio. Lately, though, his mom felt like she was constantly nagging him to practice and do the work his private instructor assigned him to do between lessons. It was putting a strain on their relationship, and they were both frustrated. *He* was annoyed that she was on him about it all the time, and *she* was angry that they were spending the money on something he had insisted he wanted, and now he wasn't doing the work.

On March 13, 2020, Gavin's music school–like so many schools and youth programs across the country–shut down due to the coronavirus pandemic, and his guitar lessons were moved online. Gavin didn't practice his lessons and assignments any more than he had before, but his mom noticed that he was playing more often and that he was attempting increasingly complicated songs. He picked up his guitar now that he had more free time at home and searched for a YouTube tutorial or online sheet music for songs he wanted to learn to play. He began teaching himself to play all the songs he'd always wanted to try but hadn't been able to because his instructor was calling the shots. He began to play with his music purely for pleasure, and he fell in love again.

Gavin's music had become a stressor–a chore. Once he started picking up the guitar more often for fun, he and his parents decided to suspend his formal lessons for a while so he could just play again. Gavin's enjoying it more than ever, and he and his mom aren't fighting about music anymore.

When you give your sons as many opportunities to play and explore new things as you can from the time they're young, they have time to discover their likes and skills. They'll build an internal gratification from discovering they're good at something, whether it's building with magnetic blocks at five, coding video games at ten, or playing the guitar at fifteen. They'll enjoy and treasure the things they're passionate about.

I know that I work, parent, and teach better when I'm able to strike a healthy balance between work and play, don't you? We could all use a little more play in our lives. Just the other day, when we had our friends over for our weekly playdate, I shut down my computer completely and drank coffee on the deck with my friends–the kids' mamas. We switched over to wine as we dug burgers out of the freezer because the visit was so pleasant they were staying past dinnertime and we'd already eaten all the food I'd put out for lunch and snacks. I took the whole day off from work and visited with my friend, played with the kids, and relaxed.

Your sons will learn that balance too, when you give them the opportunity to choose how they use their time once chores and school work are done. They will be a happier, stronger, more content and successful adults if they learn to mix work and pleasure now.

The amazing thing about play is that it leads to so many learning opportunities and gives us the chance to really become students of our own children to see what makes them tick. And those things we notice our sons are falling in love with become the things we can nurture a passion for so that they can grow in confidence and resiliency, building a strong emotional intelligence along the way.

Takeaways

- Some crucial lessons can't be taught in school or by other adult-directed means; they can only be learned through free, self-directed play. Play helps kids build strength, confidence, and emotional regulation.

- Unstructured play and downtime give children the opportunity to develop passions, interests, and competencies of their own choosing and significantly lowers their stress.

- Normal learning happens through play because kids are wired to discover and adapt to their environment.

- Overly involved parents can erode their children's confidence, unintentionally reinforcing the idea that they're not in control of their own lives and that things happen *to* them, instead of them making things happen.

▶ If you want your sons to grow to be resilient and emotionally strong, you need to encourage autonomy and experimentation

▶ Following your sons' lead can be scary.

▶ Your sons will be happier, stronger, more content and successful adults if they learn to mix work and pleasure now.

Chapter Five

Studying Our Sons

To take children seriously is to value them for who they are right now rather than adults-in-the-making.

—Alfie Kohn

Shawna's youngest son has a life-threatening immunological condition. He shows grit every single time he needs a blood test (which is at least once every two months, and he is terrified of them). One morning, he refused to get out of the car and was almost in tears as he and his mom made their way up the elevator to the doctor's office. Terrible mornings are not uncommon, and this boy has been through a lot–appointments, setbacks, struggles, pain, and more. On this morning, when he was around eleven years old, another child was in the waiting room and also struggling.

As soon as he and his mom got into the office, they heard a little girl panicking. It was hard to miss. Without missing a beat and without thinking about what he was doing, he walked over to her, sat down, and reassured her that it was all going to be OK. Shawna was stunned to see him set aside his own fears to help someone else.

"Caring," "comforting," "affectionate," "attentive," "nurturing"–these are all words that most people think of as *feminine*. Likewise, "tough," "stoic," "strong," "leader," and "rugged" bring up thoughts of masculinity. Many of our sons, especially as they get into the tween and teen years, will shy away from sharing their feelings or empathizing with others because it feels "girly" to them. If we want our sons to develop their emotional intelligence, we need to help by meeting them where they are and reframing our own expectations, as well as dispelling beliefs they're picking up from books, movies, and society about what growing to be a man is all about.

Shawna is amazing at this, and her son was able to use what he's learned about being a good person from his mama in this emotionally charged situation. Teaching our boys that loving other people is the most honorable, courageous, and manly thing they can do is the first step in crushing those stereotypical norms.

Being a strong man isn't being someone who fights, shows anger, or holds in his emotions. Being a man is being strong, courageous, empathetic, understanding and feeling one's own emotions while understanding the emotions of others. We want our boys to be authentic, to be themselves, and that means fully embracing all of their emotions.

We can help them challenge those often-implied myths, letting our sons know it's imperative to feel deeply, work hard, stand up for what's right, solve problems, and be resilient by being there for them. And even more importantly, boy moms should notice what their sons are drawn to, love, struggle with, and choose. I wrote earlier that we need to be students of our children, and if that's the only thing you take away from this book, I'll have done my job. The absolute best parenting comes when we're completely in tune with our kids.

Knowing Your Sons

I recorded a podcast interview last year with Andrew Peterson, singer, songwriter, and author of *The Wingfeather Saga*. While we were talking, the topic of being a student of your child came up. For that reason, it's still one of my all-time favorite interviews I've ever done.

Andrew spoke of a time when his band was prepping for a tour and they needed a new drummer. He talked about it at home in the evenings with his family, and one night his wife told him to look up and *notice* their son Asher. Andrew said that his wife was such a wonderful student of their children, and she regularly opens his eyes to what's in front of him.

In this case, once he took notice, he realized that his son had been practicing his drumming relentlessly. He'd perfected every song Andrew and his band was to perform onstage, and had been hoping his dad would see that he was ready to tour with the band. When Andrew took their son aside after talking it through with his wife, he said that his boy's eyes lit up at the thought of being able to travel with his dad and the band, and to be a working part of it all onstage.

Once they hit the road, after his mom told him he'd have to work hard at the job of being a musician while keeping up with his school work, Asher was tireless. He played well and as successfully as any traveling adult bandmate, and he did his school work at a little table in the tour bus when they traveled from city to city. And Andrew gained an amazing experience with his son he wouldn't have if his wife hadn't been watching.

Letting go and allowing free play and exploration, all while truly watching and getting to know our sons allows us to empower them to seek and discover passions, character traits, and skills that can carry them through their lives. Shawna's son was taught to watch and nurture because his mom is always doing that for him, and Andrew's son got a taste of what being a professional musician was like right alongside his father because his mother was in tune to him.

No two boys–even brothers being raised in exactly the same way–are the same. I look at my own children and am often amazed at the different gifts, talents, skills, beliefs, attitudes, needs, desires, passions, and interests they all have. These differences are what make mothering sons so exciting *and* frustrating all at the same time. And, while I know in my heart that each of my boys is a unique person, born for a purpose, it is so much easier to value and appreciate the aspects of my sons that are similar to me–the characteristics I can fully understand.

Have you ever thought to yourself, *"I just can't figure out where he comes from. He's so different than the rest of the family"*?

No? That's just me?

In the day to day of mothering our boys, it's easy to forget that they're still children. When we're raising more than one kiddo, it's even tougher to remember that they're each unique with their own actions, interests, and reactions to what's going on in their world. I know that I am often overwhelmed with being busy and think of my collective four as the kids, forgetting to parent each one in the way they're meant to be parented. For example, I know that one of my kids craves physical connection. If that child is acting out or melting down, it's usually a sign that he needs hugs, cuddles, or even some roughhousing and wrestling. Another craves conversation, so I'm often up late with that child, talking and talking (and talking some more).

Because each child has such different needs, it's crucial that we really and truly take the time to get to know each of our children for who they are. How effective a parent you are is a direct reflection of how well you know, understand, and respect your sons. Many parents think that their job is to cast a vision for the kind of people their children should be, then working as hard as they can to push them toward that vision, cramming their sons into a mold of their own making.

Instead, why not empower them to create their own molds as unique as they are? We're called as parents to take the time to discover the inborn uniqueness of each of our children. Parenthood isn't about raising our children to be who we think they should become. It's about raising whole sons, observing them, being alert to their needs, wants, passions, and interests, and nurturing them to be the adults they're meant to be.

Even when we recognize our sons' unique characteristics, we don't always do anything about it. Too often, we don't even tell them that we appreciate them for what makes them interesting. When was the last time you told your sons that you appreciated something about their personality, opinion, way of doing things (especially if it is different from how you would have done it), or talents? Try this: go out of your way to pay your sons at least one compliment about something that makes them unique before you go to bed tonight.

Better yet, make it a habit. I keep a little journal that is divided into different sections–one for each of my four children. I don't carry it with me constantly, but it sits on my desk or I throw it in my purse when we're on the go. When I notice a child caring for a friend, trying something new, doing a good deed, overcoming a challenge, pushing through a hard conversation, standing up for a friend, or even showing focused interest on a topic or school subject, I write it down. I don't do anything fancy; I just jot down a word or phrase to remind me so that I can bring it up in conversation or find something related to do with him.

During the early weeks of the COVID-19 pandemic shutdowns, my oldest son Trevor looked up anything and everything he could find on the current virus and past pandemics and plagues. I noticed and queued up documentaries on YouTube and Curiosity Stream and ordered him a few books about the topic. As Trevor has processed his thinking by talking it out with (or at) anyone who will listen, we've had endless conversations about the current virus and past methods of coping with plagues. He joked one day that "if we are required to wear masks wherever we go, I want to be like the plague doctors of the seventeenth, eighteenth, and nineteenth centuries and wear a beaked mask and stuff the beak with herbs or oils."

I bought him a plague doctor mask, and mama, the joy it brought him was totally worth every penny. When he looks back on this time of uncertainty and forced staying at home while all his outside activities were canceled, he's going to remember that moment of connection.

Connecting with our sons through noticing the things they love and do and are good at builds a rapport with them and fosters their emotional intelligence. Remember, a strong emotional intelligence is a better predictor of future success than intellect, and so we want our kids to know they're valued, loved, and wanted.

Letting Them Fail

Letting your children know they're valued, loved, wanted, and appreciated doesn't mean sheltering them. Letting your sons fail and being there for them when it happens is almost as important as setting them up for success. Actually, it is setting them up for future success.

Most of us have a fear of failure ourselves, and we hate the thought of it holding back our kids. Sure, we know that our sons will learn from their mistakes, but we loathe letting that happen. The truth is that when our kids are small, failures aren't such a big deal. Nobody is going to die because your son dragged the trash bag across the cement as he brought it to the curb, leaving a trail behind him. It's disappointing, but not life-threatening, when your son strikes out at his last at-bat in the game, stranding the winning run on third and sealing the win for the other team.

The trouble is, while no one will lose their life in either of these situations, it still feels terrifying for both boys and their moms. And as our sons get older and the consequences get scarier to include the likes of driving accidents or failed tests, it gets even more tempting to swoop in and solve problems before they happen.

Failure is a part of life, and we have the opportunity to be there for our sons while they're still living with us and to help them learn from their mistakes. Failure is productive and builds up our kids' resiliency, but only when two things are true. First, our sons need to actually learn from their failure and be motivated to try again. Second, our sons should remember that the failure they face doesn't shut down opportunities permanently.

When Trevor was in the third grade, we made a change to his math curriculum because I needed something more independent for him. He whizzed through and loved the program we chose for him. It was like a game to him, he said, and he looked forward to it every day. His scores were high, and he seemed to be on top of things, so I didn't think anything of it until I gave him a midterm test just to see how much he was retaining and if I should order the same program for our next homeschool year.

He bombed the test. He completely failed it and couldn't do most of the extra problems I offered him when I sat with him to see where everything had gone wrong. When he showed me how he'd navigated through each lesson, I realized that, while he hadn't learned the math that semester, he actually had very strong problem-solving skills.

Trevor wasn't bothered by his failing grade on the test at all, and he hadn't been looking at this math program as a collection of lessons. He'd been looking at it as a game to win. The program taught a mini lesson each day, then offered problems to solve for practice, much like any teacher- or video-taught math program. However, when a child is struggling, they can click a button to get help or hints, and Trevor had figured out how to use the hints to narrow down his answer choices, saving time and mental strain–and keeping him from learning the material solidly. Without the fear of failure, he had used trial and error and the process of elimination, and eventually, had picked up patterns in the algorithm of the program itself to know which answers would be correct next, without even needing to know what the actual problem was asking. He did eventually learn third-grade math and is now a seventeen-year-old about to start his senior year of high school concurrently with his freshman year of college, on his way toward a bachelor's degree in computer science.

Failure–and the lessons learned from it–builds resiliency and leads to success.

When Sean was fourteen, his mother, Kathy, discovered that she could set him up for constructive failure by having him cook a meal for the family each week. She reasoned that even if he just learned how to make a handful of meals independently, he'd leave the house as an adult who could prepare something other than ramen (or the likes of the canned potatoes fried in butter my husband cooked for me the first time I had dinner at his apartment). Kathy didn't just set Sean free in the kitchen with a refrigerator full of food and tell him to call her when dinner was on the table. She prepared him by looking through some easy recipe sites on the internet and planning the ingredients he needed for the meal he planned to tackle.

She taught him some skills he needed if the recipe he wanted to try called for something like lemon zest. She made mistakes. Kathy jumped in too soon, taking over when she saw Sean start to get behind in the steps of a recipe. She panicked when she thought he might cut himself. She set up some boundaries to keep herself in check so Sean could succeed or fail on his own. Either she or her husband stayed in the kitchen on the nights Sean cooked in case he had a question, but they busied themselves with something else like reading a book, washing dishes, or working. She also made sure that everyone in the family tried to eat their meals, even if the food didn't come out as well as planned. After all, the entire family is a team, and teams support one another. Sean is becoming a good, solid cook, and his siblings can't wait for their own turn in the kitchen (and Kathy is looking forward to working herself out of a job).

When we let our kids fail in small ways, they find the path toward strength and resiliency. Step back. Give feedback when asked instead of always stepping in to guide. Notice when your sons are ready to take on new responsibilities and challenges—and let them. Ask questions that help your sons reflect on what they want, who they are, what they care about, how they feel, and, ultimately, what they should do as a result.

Takeaways

▶ Teaching your boys that loving other people is the most honorable, courageous, and manly thing they can do is the first step in crushing stereotypical norms.

▶ The absolute best parenting comes when you're completely in tune with your kids.

▶ Letting go and allowing free play and exploration, all while truly watching and getting to know your sons, allows you to empower them to seek and discover passions, character traits, and skills that can carry them through their lives.

▶ How effective a percent you are is a direct reflection of how well you know, understand, and respect your sons.

▶ Parenthood is about raising *whole* sons, observing them, being alert to their needs, wants, passions, and interests, and nurturing them to be the adults they're meant to be.

▶ Connecting with your sons through the things they love and do and are good at builds a rapport with them and fosters their emotional intelligence.

▶ Failure is a part of life, and you have the opportunity to be there for your sons while they're still living with you and to help them learn from their mistakes.

Chapter Six

Building Confidence

Self-confidence is the foundation of all great success and achievement.

—Brian Tracy

It was a long drive to Virginia, and I wasn't sure this job would be a good fit for Trevor, but he had asked me to drive him there. He had just turned seventeen and had been playing around with audio and video editing for the past two years. He was quite good at it too. He'd started a freelance business about a year before this and had several clients whose podcasts he edited weekly. He also had filmed and edited several short promotional videos for homeschool curriculum companies and a subscription box company, and he'd won an online contest for special effects he'd created in a short film he shot with his siblings.

He was ready to try something bigger.

A few months before this trip, I'd taken Trevor with me to a social media conference I attend every year. I've become close friends with the founders of the conference, Cheryl and Shane Pitt, and Trevor planned to work with them to help with the audio and video while I attended sessions. They worked together like a well-oiled machine, and Trevor was in heaven because Shane loves technology and had very expensive camera equipment Trevor could play around with.

I caught Trevor out of the corner of my eye that weekend talking with bloggers, podcasters, and online course creators. He wasn't my teen son in that room, he was a professional who was networking, helping, teaching, and mentoring. One of the women he'd spent time talking to called him up one day in November and asked if he could come to Virginia, shoot video for her online music courses, and then edit the footage for her. It was a huge job and an even bigger opportunity, and so I found myself driving six hours across multiple state lines during the week between Christmas and New Year's Eve to be my son's driver and assistant camera woman.

I was stunned during that weekend to see him stand up, take on a huge job, work with equipment that was new to him, direct adults and kids alike, and truly command the room. I saw the man he was becoming, and his self-confidence commanded respect and the attention of the room.

He didn't come into this confidence accidentally. The building up of confidence is a process that begins when our sons are very young, toddling around, bumping into things and falling down, all the way throughout adulthood. The neuroplasticity of their brains is being shaped and strengthened through interactions between them and you, their father, their siblings, their friends, other adults, and even their enemies. They learn to handle disappointments, successes, and more through the series of positive and negative interactions they face throughout their childhoods. If this goes well, like Trevor, they'll gain a sense of strength, worth, and self-assurance. This will help them cope with challenges, build relationships, try new things, and stretch themselves. They develop confidence in themselves, others, and the world around them.

However, if they face too much disapproval, rejection, or overcorrection with little support or encouragement, they're more likely to be insecure, avoid new things, struggle with relationships, and be less resilient.

The Amazing Brain

Interestingly, the development of confidence depends on the social aspects of the brain, or the parts that make us uniquely human. The part of the human brain that gives us the capability to show empathy, planning, cooperation, organization, moral reasoning, and language takes time to develop, and so our sons stay dependent on us to help them formulate those skills as they grow. That dependence is a strength, as it builds relationships between parents and their children, parents and each other, families and their greater communities, and communities in the world at large.

When others are dependable, our sons learn to trust them and have faith in their own value. If this system of dependability breaks down, though, kids develop a sense of inadequacy and, sometimes, even shame as they grow. And children are at their most dependent and their most vulnerable when they're young. This is the time that that lack of relationship can negatively affect their brain development, and thus, their confidence, the most.

When our boys are young, they need loads of empathy, security, and love. It's deeply rooted in their biology to need to be cared about, and it's even more important that we let them know they're worth being cared about. I've seen children's behavior likened to the image of an iceberg with the tip that is exposed above the surface showing the behavior, and the wide, tapering base underneath being everything that has led up to that outward expression.

The analogy goes even further, in my opinion. When we show our sons again and again that they're worth caring about, that we empathize with and understand their feelings, and that we will meet their needs, we build that base wide and strong for them. This means that when parents are attuned, responsive, empathetic, nurturing, and compassionate, children will become securely attached. They feel loved. They feel heard. They feel worthy. Because of this, they have a healthier ability to soothe themselves and regulate their own emotions than children with less secure foundations. Securely attached sons will explore, be okay with separations, and recover from disappointment. They can talk about their feelings because they know they'll be heard. They're centered, rooted, and well adjusted.

They're confident.

Securing the Base

If you're reading this book and thinking about all the things you haven't done for and with your older son up until this point, and are ready to give up–take heart. I feel this way, too, with just about every book I read on parenting and education. We can always learn more and do better, and it's senseless to overfocus on the past. I've had this conversation with parents across the country. We can't do what we don't know, and so the only way to move is forward.

The beauty of parenting is that it is forgiving. Remember that the brain is changeable. Neuroplasticity means that, while a strong and secure attachment base is ideal to formulate in the early years, we can still help our sons overcome insecure attachment over time and with work. The best way to secure that base is to build up your child's confidence.

Confidence can be strengthened by focusing on five forms of caring: including, seeing, appreciating, liking, and loving. As you parent, look for little ways to show that you're interested, grateful, empathetic, respectful, affectionate, or loving. These actions will all demonstrate one of the five forms of caring. Let's explore them more deeply.

Including

My husband is a wonderful man. He is a teacher, an advocate for educators and children, and when he's done with work for the day, he's dedicated to making our home a safe and secure place. But he often has to be reminded to include our children in the things that he's doing around the house. Our sons are looking to be like the people they love. They want to work alongside us, but don't always know how to ask or join in. It's up to us to include them whenever and wherever we can.

I mentioned earlier that this spring, my husband came home from a grocery run with a dozen three-day-old chicks that he'd seen across the parking lot in the window of the local feed store. We'd talked about getting chickens in the past, but they definitely were not on the grocery list that day (well...not in *this* way). Everyone was surprised and jumped to attention when he got home to help set up a temporary habitat for them. The kids had a lot of fun playing with the baby chicks that were supposed to live in my dining room for only a few days while we waited for the coop he'd ordered to come in.

But after a few weeks, I was pretty much done. The house smelled like a barn, and the coop still hadn't come in. My husband reluctantly agreed to move them out of the house and into the attached garage and got to work setting up a space for them there. That worked for a while, and when the coop came in, just as I was excited to finally get the farm animals out of the garage and into in the yard where they belonged, an unseasonably cold weather pattern moved across the area, and we couldn't get the adolescent poultry outside just yet, according to my husband and kids.

In order to build the coop in the garage, though, my husband needed help. It was a small space to work in. We were up to eighteen chickens by this time, as a friend dropped off six more her son had gotten as an Easter gift, but that they couldn't keep in their housing development. The chickens were too big and feisty to stay where they were supposed to at all times. They hopped up on their perches and over the wall of corrugated plastic surrounding the brooding bins. There were feathers (and worse) all over the garage floor and in the coop materials.

There was too much to do, and the kids didn't seem interested in spending time in a stinky garage helping dad with his babies. I reminded my husband that our kids need to have the simplest things modeled for them sometimes. It might seem expected for a teen son to immediately jump in and help his dad build something, but when your teen boy is more of an algorithmic thinker and prefers video, audio, and programming to manual labor, exercise, and sport, you might need to invite him to take up a challenge.

So my husband asked, and our oldest took on the job and got out there right away, helping his father build the entire coop in an afternoon and settling the chickens in their home by dusk. The two men enjoyed an ice-cold pop on the deck in the setting sun, then went for a swim together.

Including our sons in big jobs, big decisions, and those moments out on the deck create a secure base from which they can grow. It anchors them, while showing them that their thoughts have value. Their contributions have value. Their presence has value.

Seeing

This practice of including our sons feeds right into their need to be seen, another form of caring. Being seen is a core human need, but often that old paradigm of *children should be seen and not heard* snuffs out the true meaning of what being seen is. It reduces children to subjects rather than autonomous beings with voices of their own.

Being seen is being heard.

Your sons are people and they, like all people, need to be seen *and* heard. Taking the voice of your sons away from them takes away the control they have over their lives. This leads to a dependency on authority (or someone telling them what to do all the time) instead of empowering them to control themselves, their attitudes, and their behaviors.

One of the biggest gifts I've been given over the course of my homeschooling adventures and the opportunities I've had to meet homeschoolers from around the world is observing firsthand what happens when children are truly seen and heard. When their voices matter and they have a say in their upbringing, education, and free time, magic happens. Kids feel included, seen, appreciated, liked, and loved. They feel needed.

Have you ever been to a baseball game? One of my favorite things to do is watch the big jumbo screen pan the crowd throughout the game and when the inning changes. I love how excited everyone is as soon as they realize they're on-screen. It doesn't matter how bored they were before the camera hit them, or if they'd felt like drifting off to sleep because the game was dragging. When their face hits the big screen, they jump up and down, wave excitedly, and give their friend a high five or their spouse a kiss.

Why is this?

It goes back to that need to be seen. Our boys are looking for ways to express their personhood and know that they are important enough to be recognized and appreciated by others. Good parents–like you–receive this message and show them through words, actions, and touch that they are valued.

You validate them through your words.

You empathize with them.

You appreciate them.

Appreciating

And, appreciating our sons is the third form of caring we can use to build that foundation so that our boys grow to be more confident and competent.

It had been a long day. I'd been working on a project and trying hard to get it all wrapped up before the weekend so I could focus on my kids without interruption for a few days. I'd just finished and walked into the family room where piles of laundry I'd folded on an earlier break from work still sat in stacks on the coffee table.

I sat down and buried my head in my hands and cried. As I sat there, tears flowing and weariness seeping into my bones, I felt tiny hands begin rubbing my back. "It's okay, Mommy. You did a lot of work today. You're tired. I'll rub your back until you're ready to bring the laundry upstairs, and I'll help," my then six-year-old Isaac rubbed my back for a few more minutes. When I looked up, his eyes locked on mine. "Thank you for working so we can go to the park tomorrow."

When we show our kids the ways we appreciate their efforts, they mirror that back to us. Empathy shines from their hearts. They are appreciated for who they are and they start to show you that you are too in little ways: notes left in your bag when you're traveling, coffee poured and waiting, or a simple back rub when you need it most.

Liking

Look for little ways to show your appreciation for your kids so they can reciprocate. Tell them you like what they're doing around the house, for a friend, in a game they're playing, or with a certain skill they're developing. Liking your sons, their actions, and their deeds and letting them know it is the next level of caring really begins securing that foundation we were talking about earlier in the chapter. And when your sons are included, feel seen, are appreciated, and know they're liked, this all leads to a deep feeling of being loved by the person who matters most–you.

Loving

The base of your sons' confidence needs to be solid and continually reinforced. Think about how often doubt rears its head in your mind, and multiply that for your boys. Work together to notice when someone is interested, friendly, empathetic, grateful, affectionate, or loving to you throughout the day. This is going to be a challenge for your sons, and not necessarily something they'll be able to articulate, but it is a chance for you to lead by example. Practice saying things like, "Did you see how Daddy had coffee ready for me this morning when I came downstairs? I felt so loved; it was a nice way to start my day." Or, "Miss Kristina sent me a text today. It brought me to tears. She said that she just wanted me to know that she's grateful I'm in her life." Tell your sons how these and other little things make you feel.

Noticing acts of caring for our boys will help them begin to notice too. They'll build stronger relationships with those around them–particularly their family members–because they'll see all the small acts of caring that happen to them regularly. Each experience builds memories that foster a core belief that they are valued, liked, and loved, and this secures that solid base for true confidence.

Don't Let Him Be Hard on Himself

Loving my kids hasn't just been good for them, it's been good for me too. For me, this is one of the most amazing things about being a mother. Like me, many of you reading this book may have had childhoods that weren't ideal, and while healing from past wounds are not the focus of this book, it's important to note that in the journey to becoming a better parent we tend to also revisit some of the less-than-ideal parts of our own pasts. It's a beautiful thing, though, if we allow ourselves to lean into it, that by giving what we didn't get, we can receive the good alongside our child–and perhaps heal a bit along the way. There is something restorative about treating your children as you wish you had been treated. It's like a mending of your soul, and an affirmation that you are valuable and can love unconditionally.

Now it's time to help your sons deal with those voices in their heads that tell them they're not good enough. You know what I'm talking about, don't you? Think about a time when you were mistreated. What were your immediate reactions? Did you lash back out at the person? Did you shrink back and not say anything? What were you feeling? Hurt? Anger? Stunned disbelief? Once you began to recover from the initial onslaught of feelings, what happened then?

It's common to feel a second wave of emotions after the initial ones calm down. This next wave can trigger a new internal dialogue where you're thinking about all the things you could have or should have said in the moment. You replay the event over and over in your mind, reliving it and the feelings associated with it. Think about it like a boxer's one-two punch. That first punch is the one thrown at you from outside forces, while the second punch is the one you throw at yourself. I've lost so much sleep in my lifetime throwing second, third, fourth punches at myself and more. And I suspect you have too.

How many times have you perseverated on a minor misunderstanding you had with a friend or your husband? Or overthought the activities and events leading up to a time when you were overlooked or slighted, wondering what you could have done differently to avoid it? How long have you held on to grudges or resentments long after you should have allowed yourself to soften and forgive? It's up to us to try to help our sons break that cycle of self-loathing and blame when something goes wrong, while fully recognizing that it is within human nature to do that to ourselves. These extra punches we throw at ourselves are the source of so much unnecessary suffering, making us more upset than we need to be and causing us to say and do things we'll regret later.

To some extent we can help our sons avoid experiencing many of those first punches altogether. We can create a calm and supportive environment in our homes, spend less time around difficult family members or acquaintances, and increase the activities that foster feelings of peace and love in our sons.

I'll never forget the feeling of the first Christmas Day we chose not to go to my family's big Christmas dinner. Our decision to stay home and spend a quiet Christmas with just our eight-year-old son and two-year-old and four-month-old daughters was not popular. Many of my extended family members made their opinions known, and my parents were downright angry. It was the absolute right thing to do for our son, though.

Holidays had been stressful for him most of his life. They were loud, unpredictable, and full of smells, sounds, and activities that were out of his norm. Trevor was extreme when he was young–an extreme thinker, talker, mover, and doer. Everything felt like it was on steroids with him, and so he spent most family gatherings being yelled at or corrected by one well-meaning family member after another. Parties weren't about the event we were celebrating for us anymore, they were afternoons or evenings filled with us performing damage control.

That first Christmas we spent at home was such a gift to all of us. It was quiet. We ate breakfast casseroles put together the night before that had baked while we opened gifts. Then, my husband and I sat around the family room sipping coffee and watching the kids play with their toys while the baby slumbered in her Moses basket. The afternoon was filled with Christmas carols, games, and laughter, followed by a big dinner. We capped off the night with leftover ham sandwiches and pie late in the evening before everyone curled up to sleep with new stuffed animals. It's been ten years since that first Christmas at home, and we've never gone back to leaving our home on the holidays. It was a choice that created security for our son and has led to beautiful rituals we look forward to and cherish as a family.

This isn't to say that we've sheltered our kids from all gatherings, the expectations that go along with them, or the punches that come when you're on display at an emotionally charged event and people are watching for you to make a mistake. We just choose to set our kids up for many successes before we throw all the punches at them at once. Small get-togethers to exchange gifts with cousins and aunts and uncles, then bigger activities. Our favorites are the activities that don't fall on the day of–birthday celebrations the weekend after a birthday, Christmas gift exchanges the week after Christmas, or the family holiday gathering a weekend before the holiday. We help them have small successes, then work them up to bigger displays of these skills. Scaffolding is a great strategy for creating a loving and safe place for our sons (especially those impulsive ones who are just...*more*) to encounter those first punches, so they don't continue to beat themselves up too much afterward.

We can't stop all the punches though. Sometimes your son stubs his toe and it hurts. A lot. His best friend will get mad at him for something he did or didn't do. Someone will yell at him, and he'll feel startled and angry. He'll feel what he feels and it'll be valid. Try to help him engage his mind in what he's feeling.

Teach him to be *with* the experience by riding it out and noting what he's feeling in the moment. Is his heart beating faster? Does he have thoughts swirling around or is his mind blank? Are his hands clenching together as the fight, flight, or flee response tells him to fight? Help him accept these feelings with curiosity and self-compassion–kind of like a scientist observing a subject.

Then help him let go of the tension he's feeling. Show him how to relax his muscles or replace intrusive thoughts with calmer ones. Show him how to take deep breaths, breathing in through his nose and out through his mouth. Teach him to stretch out his arms and hands to release that clenched-up feeling. Teaching him to release tension and let go of unhealthy thoughts and emotions is a gift your son will use his entire life.

Finally, help your son draw in what would benefit him in moments like these so he learns to replace what is negative with what is good and beneficial. Improving self-talk, reframing what he is thinking, and changing perspectives are all strategies he can use now and in his future any time one of those punches comes his way.

The most important thing you can do for your son is to help him see that those little mishaps and disappointments that happen along the way are a natural and unavoidable part of life. He can't control all the things he will experience, but he can control how he reacts to them. If the brand-new roller-coaster he has looked forward to riding all summer long is closed for maintenance on the day you were finally able to take him to the amusement park, it stinks. It's a huge disappointment. It makes for a big letdown, but there's no sense in letting it completely ruin the day. There are other coasters to ride and treats to eat. If he accepts that first disappointment for what it is–a setback–then it's like a drain plug stopping the flow of water and interrupting the replays that will lead your son down the spiral of all those self-inflicted sucker punches.

Taking Down Your Child's Inner Critic

It's useful to have perspective on those setbacks that happen as a natural part of life. For example, most of us care about how others see us. We feel unsettled if others are critical of us. The priority that we place on what others think of us leads to embarrassment, shame, and hurt. It leaves us vulnerable. These are a normal pain of living and can lead to great things like activism and altruism. When our sons continue to beat themselves up, though, after the initial point of pain, they can begin to feel lonely, envious, resentful, and indignant. They can lose their focus and strength and give in to disenchantment.

Building on this, teach your sons to take a step back and breathe. Help them recognize that focusing on the negative feelings or what they could have done or said better is needless suffering that will only lead to worse. Guide your child to recognize that inner critic we all have. The little voice inside that focuses on our imperfections and causes us to give up is there for everyone, even if we feel it only talks to us.

There are two key voices inside all people. One nurtures us. The other tears us down. One speaks kindness while the other criticizes. Both of these voices are important to a person's normal development. The nurturer teaches our sons to have self-compassion. It encourages them. It allows them to trust themselves and move forward with confidence. The critic can be good for our sons too. It can help them see where they've gone wrong. It helps them see how they can make amends and turn things around. It drives the empathy that is important to developing emotional intelligence.

Unfortunately, the inner critic can easily, and often, go too far. The critic can become insidious, nit-picking, shaming, scolding, and continue to find fault after fault within our sons. It becomes big, powerful, and oppressive. It weighs them down. The inner critic can completely outweigh the nurturer, rendering it small and useless. This tears down our sons' self-worth and shames them, affecting their mood and resilience, leading to an endless cycle of self-shame and poor self-esteem.

There are ways to combat the inner critic, though. Our boys need to understand the cycle of self-criticism and notice when they are unfair to themselves. Help them talk about and identify their pain and needs, and to stand up for their rights. Help them notice when they become angry at themselves, and talk to them about turning it around. Tell them to listen for a berating or shaming tone in the way they talk to themselves in their minds. Help them label it as criticism. Remind them that their pain does matter and that you're there for them when they're feeling down.

When our boys are mindful of their self-talk, they can learn from that and work on being kinder to themselves. They stop identifying with the negativity and realize that those thoughts are not truths about them. This shores up and strengthens their inner nurturer–the ally they need to beat down the critic.

When they've strengthened their inner nurturer, our sons are protected and encouraged when others are critical of them because they taught themselves to believe in the good.

The best news about this is that we can play a critical role in strengthening our boys' inner nurturer, mamas. Beginning when they're very young, they develop their nurturer based on how outside nurturers tend them. The more we praise, support, and love on our sons, the stronger their nurturer becomes. When the inner critic gets loud or life gets challenging, tell your sons to call on their nurturer.

Encourage your sons to be wary as soon as they recognize the inner critic begin to speak up. Its voice is not to be trusted. Help them make the choice to separate from it. Help them doubt the words the critic speaks. Show them how the inner critic grows and gets stronger when others are mean. What other kids say and do to be hurtful is wrong, and it is wrong for your sons to be mean to themselves too.

Takeaways

▶ Your sons' dependence on you is a strength that builds relationships between you and the communities in the world at large.

- It's deeply rooted in your sons' biology to need to be cared about, and it's even more important that you let them know they're worth being cared about.

- When parents are attuned, responsive, empathetic, nurturing, and compassionate, children will become securely attached. They feel loved. They feel heard. They feel worthy.

- Strengthen confidence by focusing on five forms of caring: including, seeing, appreciating, liking, and loving.

- Including your sons and showing them that their thoughts have value anchors them. Their contributions have value. Their presence has value.

- Your boys are looking for ways to express their personhood and know that they are important enough to be recognized and appreciated by others.

- Noticing acts of caring for your boys will help them begin to notice too.

- There is something restorative about treating your children as you wish you had been treated.

- Your boys need to understand the cycle of self-criticism and notice when they are unfair to themselves.

- When've they strengthened their inner nurturer, your sons are protected and encouraged when others are critical of them because they taught themselves to believe in the good.

Part Three

Fostering Relationships

*Children belong in families, which,
ideally, serve as a sanctuary and
a cushion from the world at large.
Parents belong to society and are a
part of that greater world. Sometimes
parents are a channel to the larger
society, sometimes they are a shield
from it. Ideally, they act as filters,
guiding their children and teaching
them to avoid tempting trash.*

—Louise Hart, PhD

Do you remember feeding your baby boy, and as he sat in that high chair and opened his mouth wide to take in the spoon, you opened yours too? Have you ever yawned when someone else yawned? (Are you yawning now?) Have you started smiling as you walked into the playroom and heard peals of little boy laughter as your sons bonded over some game play or another? According to Daniel Siegel and Tina Payne Bryson in their book, *The Whole-Brain Child: 12 Revolutionary Strategies to Nurture Your Child's Developing Mind*, scientists call this "emotional contagion." This is when the internal states of others, like joy, fear, playfulness, sadness, or anger directly affect our own states of mind and behaviors. We pull others into our inner worlds and they pull us into theirs.

This, according to Siegel and Payne, is why neuroscientists call the brain a social organ. We are biologically wired to be in relationships with others and understand where they are coming from. We grow and become better–or worse–because of the people we have relationships with. That means that the kinds of people our kids develop relationships with throughout their lives are literally shaping the people they are becoming. Relationships form the foundation for how they relate to others for the rest of their lives.

When our sons are young, it's important that we surround them with people who'll help them grow in character and exemplify behavioral traits that are healthy, and that we widen their circle as they grow. In *Raising Boys: Why Boys Are Different–and How to Help Them Become Happy and Well-Balanced Men*, Steve Biddulph explains that boys go through three stages as they grow and mature, and during these stages have varying needs. From about birth to age six, he writes, boys tend to have strong relationships with their mothers. This is when they start growing that strong base–a foundation of love and security that's warm and safe.

While they don't need their mothers any less, during the second stage of boyhood, between ages six and fourteen, according to Biddulph, boys are looking more toward being whatever it means to be a man. They look toward their father for interests and activities during these years. This is the time our sons are gaining confidence, competence, kindness, compassion, and playfulness. They're learning to be a well-rounded and balanced person.

Finally, in their third stage, boys from ages fourteen to adulthood need input from nonparental adult mentors who share great morals and can help our sons become compassionate members of society. Biddulph reminds us that our sons don't pass through these stages abruptly from one to another, and they never really forfeit the need for a relationship with mom and dad, which is the foundation on which resiliency and emotional intelligence are built. Rather, they overlap one another and grow together. These stages just give us a ballpark so we know what our sons need at various ages when it comes to helping them grow strong relationships and connections.

When our sons spend their time with the most important people in their lives and we remain cognizant of the developmental stage they're in, they develop critical skills like communicating, listening, interpreting nonverbal expressions, and learning to share and sacrifice. They also start to see where they fit in the world around them and how successful relationships work.

Chapter Seven

Family Connections

Families are the compass that guides us. They are the inspiration to reach great heights, and our comfort when we occasionally falter.

—Brad Henry

Fox was about three years old when his mom Cheryl worked as a babysitter for a family. He'd tag along and hang out with her and the kids. This family also had a sweet older lady named Mrs. Coates come by often to help with their laundry. Mrs. Coates was in a terrible car accident that resulted in severe bruising from the top of her head all the way down her body. She looked battered and swollen, which was scary to the children Cheryl watched.

One day while waiting for a load to finish so she could fold clothes, Mrs. Coates sought Cheryl out, tears glistening. She told Cheryl that while she sat resting, sweet little Fox had come over to her silently, placed his hand on her cheek, and looked deeply into her eyes. Mrs. Coates was touched by his empathy and care. Fox didn't see an ugly old woman covered in bruises, or as she liked to say, "a giant walking hematoma." He saw someone weary, in pain, and feeling down. Those chubby preschool fingers, warm on her face, and the connection emanating from his heart touched Mrs. Coates and brought her to tears.

Connection reminds us that we'll be okay no matter how hard things get. It gives us security. It allows us to take chances, be brave, and know we're loved. It helps us let others know they can turn to us when they're hurting, and helps us know that we can ask for help when we need it.

However, connection is not just about getting through tough times together. It gives us greater security. It gives us a base, brings us joy, and lets us draw closer to our potential. When we take time to build a strong connection with our children, we let them know that we're completely in love with them, will do anything for them, and will support them in any way we can. It gives them the strength and example to forge strong connections with others and go on to develop amazing relationships of their own.

Our sons gain an essential feeling of belonging from connection, starting from their infancy, when we were the center of their universe, to a continuously widening circle as they grow and take their place in the larger community. It's easy to feel the importance of their dependency when they're small, but it gets more and more difficult to reconcile that forging new relationships and stepping away from us to find other mentors and influences is a natural and normal part of adolescence. These outside connections build trust.

When boys are able to spend time with others who care for them and will support them, they gain security. This is essential if we want them to be resilient. Without a strong foundation and an ever-widening circle, kids are reluctant to take risks or try new things. If they don't push themselves to take risks, they'll become more timid, more afraid.

Our sons need many different circles of connection in order to feel secure, needed, understood, and protected. We don't want them to form theses connections without some guidance because it's important to know and trust the people our kids spend time with, but we need to be careful not to instill anxiety in our kids. Most people are good, and we want our kids to be smart while knowing that the greater community is filled with people worth knowing.

I recently recorded a podcast interview with Blake Boles, author of several books and an expert in nontraditional learning, specifically self-directed education. He said that one of the most effective ways for teens to get ahead and learn things they're interested in knowing about is to shoot an email to an expert and ask if they can spend some time with them. He points out that very few experts in a field are not interested when a young teen has the confidence to send an unsolicited email asking to learn about that which the expert is passionate about. He almost always says yes.

When I first pulled Trevor out of school to homeschool, I didn't know any other homeschoolers in my area. We went to every activity I could find that I thought he'd be interested in because I wanted him to love learning and make new homeschooled friends. At eight, he became the youngest member of a local astronomical association because we went to all their events and his questions were so intelligent. When he asked if he could join, they let him. When we teach our sons to avoid strangers, we rob them of the possibility of making connections that may enrich their lives.

Begin with Empathy

Forming any kind of lasting connection needs to start with empathy. It's critical in forming relationships with others. It's important to note what empathy isn't though. It isn't sympathy. Empathy isn't when we feel sorry for others. Empathy, at its core, is when we *walk a mile in someone else's shoes*. Have you heard that saying before? It's a good one to remember. Empathy is all about trying to feel what another person is feeling. It's about withholding judgment until you've thought about it from the other person's perspective. Empathy also doesn't mean understanding what another person is going through. The truth is that we may never completely understand, but we can try to grapple with what another person might be feeling. It's being able to say, "I can't imagine what that must have been like. I'm so sorry," and offering them that truth along with warmth and comfort.

When we model empathy by showing it to our sons, we let them know that their experiences and perspectives are important, and we show them firsthand how to act toward others to form lasting, *real* relationships. Too often we put expectations on our sons that are unfair. We treat them as extensions of ourselves or as little beings to be trained, and we can't imagine that they have real problems. We think, *how can he be so upset about a misunderstanding with the neighbor kiddo? This doesn't compare to my pay cut at work. How can he be crying over a skinned elbow when his best friend is dealing with childhood cancer?* I know that sometimes I'm tempted to tell my sons to let it go or to just get over it because I get caught up in the busy.

But our sons' problems are just as real and valid as our own, and if we're not modeling empathetic listening then they're not learning how to do it. If we fall into a pattern of minimizing their struggles, or worse, belittling and shaming them for feeling that way, we shut down their willingness to come to us for support.

Boys need to be seen and heard–on their terms and about their issues. Boyhood has plenty of challenges, and adults need to work to remember back to their own childhood with honesty and empathy toward the children they once were. Boys need empathy, but more than that, they need to see the adults in their lives project and model that empathy for them so that they can become caring adults. When they struggle to care and see things from another's perspective, they grow into adults who struggle to form lasting relationships with others.

Showing empathy toward our sons provides them with both security and support. We essentially create a sort of safety net for them where they know they'll be listened to and validated, and they also know they can get help. They'll share their struggles freely because they understand that they won't be belittled or shamed. They'll seek our help when they make mistakes because they know we will support them without censure.

Because this is a book about developing resiliency and emotional intelligence in our sons, I want to take a moment to really impress the importance of teaching them that we'll be empathetic to them when they show emotions. I can't overemphasize the value in encouraging our boys, particularly, to show their emotions.

You might think that today's society, with all its push for equality, would have nothing more to work on in regard to boys showing emotions. That *of course* boys should cry when they feel hurt or sad and show joy, embarrassment, fear, and any other emotion they're feeling when they feel it. But studies continue to show that adults react differently to boys than girls at the earliest of ages.

Girls are cuddled, cooed to, and held more. Boys are bounced, wrestled with, and left to cry it out more often. Boys are told to shake off an injury. They're told to be tough when they cry. Their fears are minimized and they're told to "just ignore them and be brave."

These attitudes are in complete opposition to empathy. Adults who do this, often unconsciously, fail to see things from their son's perspective, and they're shaming him for being discontent.

When we force our sons to disconnect from their very real and completely justified feelings, we deny our sons the important skill they need to build relationships and recover from setbacks in their lives.

Revolutionary Masculinity

It's tough, though. Boys often act in ways that further feed the misconception that their inner emotions are less intense than those of our daughters. Girls naturally talk (sometimes endlessly as you mamas who have both boys and girls, like me, know) about their friendships, their feelings, and the drama of their days, and they seek us out to fill us in on all of it. Our sons often downplay an issue or pretend not to notice they weren't invited to a party or into the Minecraft server their teen group set up. Girls react passionately to injustices and challenge us directly by yelling or fighting for their independence or freedom to stay up late, go to a friend's, or talk online until the wee hours of the night. Our sons act like they don't care. They withdraw, become silent, shrug things off, and act tired or even like they can't hear us talking to them. Generalizations about girls being girls and boys being boys are wrong, but the patterns in their behaviors often reinforce our preconceived notions that boys feel less deeply than girls.

In fact, the opposite is likely true. Well, not necessarily that boys feel more than girls, but that they feel just as intensely as they do. Research suggests that the rich inner life of boys is stifled by these societal prejudices as they go through their tween and teen years. According to Niobe Way, author of the book *Deep*

Secrets: Boys' Friendships and the Crisis of Connection, late elementary and early middle school-aged boys talk about the depth of their friendships and the love they feel toward their friends. They talk about being listened to and the importance of having someone who knows everything there is to know about them. As they get older, though, they talk more about buddies than friends. They describe their friendships from a more activity-centered perspective than a meaningful relationship. In fact, they tend to have grown into the perspective that the types of relationships they once had with their friends are less than manly and more feminine.

I don't know about you, mama, but I want my sons to develop and hold lasting friendships that are meaningful, deep, connected, and real. I want to live in a world where we don't condition our sons to believe that shutting down and holding back their feelings is a sign of manhood. I want the world to nurture and build up all boys to know that an essential characteristic of true masculinity is to be empathetic and sensitive to those around them. That this sensitivity will enable them to grow to be better coworkers, friends, lovers, husbands, and fathers. I want my sons to nurture the next generation of kind, loving fathers who will do the work of their sons and so on and so forth. I want my boys to grow up as revolutionaries in a world where men benefit from growing meaningful relationships and connections within their family and the greater community.

This revolutionary masculinity would position our men to be more resilient in the most challenging of times because they won't need to know everything and be everything to everyone. They'd be solidly grounded in their strengths and appreciate that their weaknesses are the strengths of others so they would reach out for help when it's needed.

This strength of self is what makes a man tackle hard times with his head held high, knowing he can take care of those he loves because he's secure knowing what he's good at and with letting the ones he loves soar in the areas that they're strongest in.

Feel, Fix, and Try Again

We can't change the world alone, nor can we shield our sons from all forms of prejudice and stereotypes society will throw at them, but we can ensure that we're creating a space in our homes where our sons can freely and fully express their emotions. We can start, as Niobe Way tells us, by knowing those emotions are there. Our sons have a deep, rich inner life full of feelings, even if they aren't sharing it with us. Use this knowledge to quell your frustration at their silence and seeming indifference. Change your perspective from *they don't care about anything* to *they need time and space to process*. This understanding allows them time to strengthen that emotional resilience rather than reinforce the stereotype that *men don't show their feelings*.

Our sons pay very close attention to how we respond to their feelings and struggles. When my kids were very little, I wanted them to know that a skinned knee, while painful, was part of the experience of learning to play hard in the summertime; biking, skating, and running all had the potential to result in skinned knees and elbows. Instinctively one summer, when my oldest was small, I celebrated his skinned knee while doctoring him up. I said, "Yay! You got your first summer scrape out of the way already! Summer is really here–hooray for embracing it. Those hurt for a bit and are so annoying. It's a good thing we stocked up on knee-sized bandages; which one would you like? Let's get this fixed up and go grab a popsicle." Getting the first summer scrape out of the way became a family conversation we've had for over a decade and a half since. Celebrating the skinned knee wasn't about minimizing the pain of the scrape, it was about registering scrapes as rites of summertime passage, validating the pain and inconvenience of it, then moving on so that my kids won't shy away from riding their bikes or climbing trees. When we validate, empathize, and react calmly, our kids take note. We're giving our sons profoundly valuable coping mechanisms for dealing with challenges: feel, fix, and try again.

Remember that boys who grow up in an empathetic and caring environment learn to be empathetic and caring. A simple "I really love and care about you. Please help me understand how you're feeling right now so I can help you" can build bridges between you and your son that will have ripple effects far beyond your home.

Connections within the Home

Bram has a special connection with his little sister Amelie. From the moment she was born, his parents noticed it. Cheryl and Shane homeschool their kids and own their own business, so they have a lot of family time together and are able to witness and nurture this sibling bond well and often. "One day," Cheryl recalls, "I was fighting horribly with Amelie over her piano practice. She was five and just didn't want to do anything I asked her to do, and we were both incredibly frustrated. Bram came into the room and asked if he could try, and since I was so angry, I told him good luck and went into the other room. Within a few minutes I heard the sound of Amelie's playing and just lost it. I went into my room and shut the door behind me and sat on my bed. I couldn't even get my daughter to practice piano–something she loves–and my nine-year-old son was doing a better parenting job than I was." Cheryl was frustrated, as we moms often get when our kids won't listen. I remember having that same feeling of failure when my then two-year-old Isaac told me that Molly (his seven-year-old sister) was his favorite mommy.

Cheryl remembers sitting in that room a while before hearing a knock on the door. She opened it and there stood Bram, who said, "Don't worry about it, Mom. Sometimes we all just need a change of scenery. You always practice with Amelie, and she just needed something different. I was that something different today, and you needed a break."

When our sons are young, especially when they're our first as Trevor was mine, we notice every little thing they do. We celebrate every milestone. We watch them at play and we tell everyone about the miracle of their development. Then they get older. Older boys get dirty more often. They rip their jeans. They fall in mud puddles. They get stuck in trees and interrupt your dinner making. They take out seventeen glasses a day and leave them all over the house. They're definitely not as cute as they were when they were babies. They're especially not fun as they begin to push us away, trying to figure out who they are and what their place is in the world.

Because our time tends to be more limited with them as they get older, we instinctively try to cram as much *important* stuff into the time we have with them as we can. We tend to try to have those big conversations with our older sons since we have less time to get it in. Instead of playing with them (which they still crave, believe it or not), we talk about transcripts, behaviors, results, and game scores, and we end up making a huge mistake.

Instead of bringing us closer to our sons, this actually serves to push them away. Talking about these things when they really just want to hang out makes time with us anxiety-producing for them. Moms, we want our sons to enjoy being with us, not regret the time they take to sit and talk. When we focus solely on our sons' classes, output, and products, *they* begin to feel like a product too. You'll have a great handle on the things they are doing, but you won't know how they're feeling anymore. You'll know the scores they achieved on the last test they took, but not what they're struggling with. You'll push them away and miss out on the beautiful joy it is to be an active parent of a teen son.

Our kids get the sense that we no longer care about who they are. They feel like all we moms want to talk about is how they are preparing for their future, and that their personal life should stay personal. I get it, mamas. I truly do. I'm a homeschool mom who spent a decade and a half teaching in the public school system. I'm acutely aware of what my sons should be achieving by the time they reach an arbitrary age. I fall into the same cycle of wishing they shared more with me–and then shutting them down when they try to so we can focus on the *important* stuff.

I can change, and so can you.

Try giving your sons the time they're craving. Play a video game with them–really. Trevor saved his money so he could buy a VR headset he'd been eyeing for a while. I'm not a fan of virtual reality, video games, or even computer programs–ironic, really, as I have an online site, podcast, membership community, and coaching program–but my teen loves them. So I try to make time to play with him a few times a week when he asks me. We have great conversations about friends, hopes, fears, and stressors while we play together. Yes, it's important to know your son's academic accomplishments, but it's more important to know about his life and what's going on inside his head.

And here's the best thing about this approach. You're not sacrificing the guidance time you might feel like you need to take with your son because when you both enjoy the time you spend together, you'll find ways to make more time together. You can spend some of this new and extra time talking about the big things since you're already spending the majority of time on the fun. And, truly, that unconditional love and joy you show when you spend time doing things your son loves doing is exactly what your son needs to have a phenomenal start to his adult life.

Family Time

Every year for all the birthdays in our house, we follow the same pattern. It's a day off for the whole family–no work, school, or chores. Now, we're lucky in that only one of our six birthdays falls when school is in session, so Daddy only has to take one personal day a year off for birthdays, and sometimes that person's birthday falls on a weekend, so he doesn't have to use up one of his precious personal days or create sub plans to stay home and celebrate. We start all birthdays the same–with cinnamon-roll-donut-hole cake and presents. What IS cinnamon-roll-donut-hole cake? Well, it's my cheater's version of monkey bread. I take three tubes of buttermilk biscuits, cut each biscuit into fourths, throw the wedges in a zip-top bag filled with cinnamon and sugar, and shake it up. Then I toss those cinnamon-sugar-coated dough wedges into a greased fluted pan and bake. When the "cake" comes out of the oven, I slather it with icing made from powdered sugar and milk, the kind you find on cinnamon rolls. The first time I made this, Trevor was two. He called it cinnamon-roll-donut-hole cake because the pieces looked like donut holes all baked together, and it all tasted like a giant cinnamon roll.

The name stuck.

This formed the base of a family ritual we all look forward to on every single birthday in the family. My kids aren't overly focused on big parties and getting together with friends, though we have done that too. They're excited to start their day with this traditional family breakfast, presents, then spending the day together doing whatever the birthday boy or girl wants to do.

Family rituals like this create shared stories and connection-building times together. And they don't have to be this big of a deal, either. You can create rituals around anything, and simple is best. Maybe you share something each of you is thankful for at dinner every night. Even something easy like preparing a meal together, taking care of pets (or in our case, the dozen and a half chickens we now have free-ranging in our backyard), or grocery shopping. These are perfect opportunities to listen to our children. We can encourage them to answer silly questions, dance in the family room together, sit out under the stars and point out constellations, or tell jokes to each other.

As your sons get older, family meals and times together become harder to schedule and manage, but make a point to schedule them in. Try for at least two nights a week where you're all having dinner together. No phones at the table and no excuses are allowed. Respect your older teen's schedules by planning with him, but hold him accountable for being there. Make it special by lighting candles. We ordered some sweet-smelling beeswax candles and ceramic holders one year and the kids love to pull those out.

When your sons are younger, other rituals include bedtime routines with storytelling or reading aloud, sharing hobbies together, and spending time one-on-one with each of your children once every week. This scheduling of one-on-one time is especially challenging when you have multiple kids, but yields so much value that it's well worth it. My husband and I have started making a point to bring one child with us each time we have to leave the house for anything, if it's at all possible. We had been feeling good about those efforts, but weren't sure if it mattered. And then the COVID-19 pandemic hit. At first, my husband would make the quick grocery runs himself and do all of our errands in short little bursts. Our kids all stayed home with me.

We started noticing greater anxiety in our children who were prone to it, and angry bursts and a quickness to frustration as time went on. It dawned on us that they were missing that connection as much as we were. We started making a point to again take one kid out each day–at first to a drive-through for a drink or to bring back ice cream for the other kids, and then, as things started opening back up, for errands that could be completed safely and easily with a child in tow. It made an incredible difference and demonstrated just what a little thing like a ride into town can do for a child's sense of belonging and worth.

Time individually with each of our kids also gives us the chance to not only understand each of them, but to help them understand each other. We can talk about how to react when a sibling is having a hard time. We can point out times when a sibling stands up for what is right and supports them.

Recently, my son was accused of saying something very mean and inappropriate to a friend's sibling. It became a downward-spiraling situation where he continued to stand his ground saying that, while he *was* unkind in his words and tone, he didn't say exactly what he was being accused of saying. My youngest daughter has special needs. She struggles with learning disabilities, processing challenges, sensory processing disorder, and debilitating anxiety. She's pretty much always frightened. In this situation, though, she stood up for her big brother. She spoke up against the injustice she saw and told what she'd witnessed, which was in opposition to what was being told, and while the other party still didn't believe her brother, she did what she felt was right and just.

When my son and I had the chance to hang out the other day, I pointed his sister's actions out to him, highlighting her loyalty.

I explained that at this point in the situation, it didn't really matter what was really said–neither party was willing to relent, each having witnesses of their own on two completely divided sides. He knows in his heart whether he was innocent or guilty of the accusations, and he'll have to live with that knowledge–either that he lied or a friend did. But the gift in this situation was seeing the loyalty his sister had shown him, even when it was a scary thing to do. Conversations about what others in the family are doing that are great, and how each of them fits into the team, can be a platform for combatting sibling rivalry and can serve to draw everyone even closer together.

There is so much out there written about sibling rivalry, so I won't waste time going into it here. I do suggest some websites and books in the Additional Resources section of this book and have direct links to each one at RaisingResilientSons.com if you need more support in this area. I will say this, though: We shouldn't focus on eradicating sibling rivalry altogether. It serves a purpose. Children learn to work things out in a loving and empathetic home by stumbling through fights and squabbles with their brothers and sisters. It's a safe way to find their individuality and independence while still being a part of the greater team.

I would suggest helping each of your kiddos find their own thing so that they have something of their own to shine in. For example, all of my kids are smart, articulate, good with younger kids, and love helping others out. Each one, though, excels in a different area. My oldest is a self-taught video and audio editor who started a business when he was 15. My second child is an incredibly talented actress and has won the starring roles in several community theater productions, including Mary

Lennox in the musical *The Secret Garden* and Anne Shirley in the play *Anne of Green Gables*. My third child is an animal whisperer and can corral chickens, calm reptiles, and train puppies easily. My youngest is an athlete who naturally kicks, throws, and runs like he's been playing for longer than he's been alive. Encouraging their different interests gives each of them a chance to star in their own galaxy, while giving the others something to cheer them on about.

Takeaways

▶ Connection reminds us that we'll be okay no matter how hard things get.

▶ When you teach your sons to avoid strangers, you rob them of the possibility of making connections that may enrich their lives.

▶ Forming any kind of lasting connection needs to start with empathy.

▶ If you fall into a pattern of minimizing your sons' struggles, or worse, belittling and shaming them for feeling that way, you shut down their willingness to come to you for support.

▶ When you force your sons to disconnect from their very real and completely justified feelings, you deny them the important skill they need to build relationships and recover from setbacks in their lives.

- Aim to want your sons to develop and hold lasting friendships that are meaningful, deep, connected, and real.

- Ensure that you're creating a space in your home where your sons can freely and fully express their emotions.

- When you validate, empathize, and react calmly, your kids take note. You're giving your sons profoundly valuable coping mechanisms for dealing with challenges. Feel, fix, and try again.

- When the time you spend with your son is something you both enjoy, you'll find ways to make more time together.

- Children learn to work things out in a loving and empathetic home by stumbling through fights and squabbles with their brothers and sisters. It's a safe way to find their individuality and independence while still being a part of the greater team.

Chapter Eight

The Greater Community

*The greatness of a community is
most accurately measured by the
compassionate actions of its members.*

—Coretta Scott King

"Hey, Mom! I need your help. Carlos is stuck in a tree and we can't get him out." Trevor was eight or nine, and his neighborhood friend Carlos was not allowed to climb trees. His dad worked from home and struggled with anxiety, so he was usually hovering nervously about but had to take some calls that afternoon, so Carlos and Trevor were playing in our yard. *Great*, I thought to myself. *Of all the kids to get stuck. I just hope I can help him down before his dad knows he was climbing trees again and forbids him to play over here.*

I went outside, expecting to see Carlos dangling on a branch or slipping down the trunk of one of the many climbing trees we had in our wooded backyard. I never would have imagined the sight that greeted me. It's one of those things you might read about in a book and shake your head at. *There's no way that could happen. This author was lazy and didn't suspend disbelief carefully enough to make it seem real. Forget this book...*

But it *was* real. And I needed to figure out what to do.

Carlos's knee was wedged solidly in the V-shape of a trunk (it was the kind of tree that splits its trunk at some point in its growth and looks like a single tree on the bottom and two separate trees on the top). He looked comfortable, at least, like he was just resting his knee in the crook of that tree. Before Trevor had gone to get me for help, he'd dragged a wrought-iron chair over to his friend so that he could stand his other foot on it, relieving some of the pressure that had been caused when he was hanging a few feet from the ground by his knee. Carlos stood in that chair calmly and played on Trevor's Nintendo 3DS while Trevor looked over his shoulder shouting directions at him.

"Did you have your Nintendo out here with you when you guys were climbing trees?" I asked.

Trevor looked at me, "No. When Carlos slipped and got stuck, we tried to get him out for a while. His knee won't budge. I figured he'd be stuck for a long time and I didn't want him to be bored so I got him the chair and my DS." My little boy took the time to see to the comfort of his friend before seeking help in the crisis. I didn't know, in that moment, whether to laugh, cry, or scream. This was such a strange situation.

I checked in with Carlos. He felt no pain in his knee. It was just stuck there and felt fine. I pushed at it. I tugged at it. I tried to pry the V-shaped trunks further apart. Nothing was working. In fact, when I pushed at Carlos's knee, that was the only time he felt any pain. There was no other choice; I had to call for help.

First, I called Carlos's dad and assured him that his son was okay, but that he was stuck in a tree. I couldn't figure out how to explain the "stuck-ness" to him over the phone, so I just let him go through the same series of incredulity I did, once he arrived. The second call I made was to the fire department. I explained the situation and told them I'd never seen anything like it before, and that they probably hadn't either. I'm pretty sure the dispatcher rolled her eyes at me when she said, "These guys have seen everything," and told me they were on their way.

While we waited, Trevor got some fruit snacks for him and Carlos to share, and Charles, his father, paced my backyard. I waited out front for the fire truck and paramedics. When they arrived, the chief, who had come along for the ride, laughed out loud. He'd never seen anything like this in his entire career and wasn't exactly sure what to do. Carlos was wedged in tightly.

As they all discussed options, Charles grew paler and paler, which was something to see as he was the darkest man I'd ever known. Looking back, I laugh every single time I picture his face when the chief mentioned breaking one of the trunks, cutting the tree down, or sawing around Carlos's knee. He kept apologizing to me, as if the potential loss of the tree was as heartbreaking as losing a child would be. Anxiety can be a funny thing.

Trevor had moved over to Charles by this time and was patting his arm or his back or whatever he could reach each time he paced back and forth. As Carlos was unperturbed and focused on the video game, we all knew he'd be fine.

Finally, the firefighters decided to try using one of the adapters they have for their "jaws of life." It's an air pad they can inflate to slowly lift cars off victims trapped underneath. They inserted it in the V above Carlos's knee and put the chief's hard helmet on Carlos's head to protect him in case any branches broke and fell. The chief held Carlos while another firefighter held his trapped knee, and they began to inflate the pad. It worked perfectly. As the pad pushed against the V-shape slightly, it created just enough space to slip Carlos's knee out and set him gently on the ground. Amazingly, there was no bruising or pain at all. Carlos had a slight imprint from where the seam of his jeans had been pressing between his knee and the tree for two hours.

Friendships change throughout childhood and adolescence. We haven't seen Carlos or Charles since we moved away from that neighborhood about eight years ago. Children need these connections to multiple groups of friends, relatives, and the community, so that when one group changes because of moves, classroom shifts, misunderstandings, or differing interests, they have other groups to fall back on. They'll always have the memories of running with different groups, getting in and out of predicaments with them, but things do change over time.

Relatives are helpful in forming relationships that can bridge the changes that happen as peer groups ebb and flow. Cousins, in particular, are amazing anchors for kids to have in their life. When your son is having a problem with a friend at school or their homeschool program, they can often open up to an older cousin more readily that their parents. Cousins can also be good motivators for children.

My oldest son is seventeen at the time of this book's release. We moved in the last year and are now closer–only fifteen minutes away–from my brother-in-law and his wife. Trevor is getting to spend a lot of time with his eighteen-year-old cousin. They've always enjoyed each other's company, but we lived about forty-five minutes from them and Liam was very active in his school's athletic program while Trevor was busy with all the activities we do as homeschoolers. Our schedules just didn't mesh well.

I've been hounding Trevor for a year and a half to work toward getting his driver's license, but he kept telling me he didn't need it as I took him anywhere he wanted to go. But spending more time with Liam and depending on his cousin to come get him anytime they want to do something is motivating him to work toward not only getting his license, but also saving for a used car. By widening the sphere of connection our sons have, we offer them the opportunity to be motivated by other good influences.

Think about ways you could surround your sons with neighbors and relatives who could be those influences on them. Perhaps your next-door neighbor's son who plays in a band and volunteers his time at an inner-city after-school program teaching music lessons could inspire your son to use his talents in a unique way. In encouraging this, you offer the older neighbor a valuable opportunity to inspire someone younger, who can look up to him. For your younger boys, you're widening their circle of connection and showing them examples of hardworking teens.

An older neighbor, uncle, grandparent, or aunt can also foster wonderful connections, giving our sons a chance to feel like they are part of something bigger than themselves. For generations, families grew up together, helping to run family businesses or farms. Boys worked alongside grandfathers and uncles and cousins. As they grew and matured, they took on more of the responsibilities and the parts of the businesses they were best suited to. As adults, many of them took over the family businesses, deepening the connections between them and their past.

It's unusual for our sons to have that extended family dynamic and business waiting to be taken over today, and we can't completely replicate that experience for them, but we can try to strengthen family connections for our kids' sake. Whether our extended family is large or small, we can encourage our sons to reach out in whatever way makes sense. We can organize family dinners and invite great aunts over or find ways to include grandparents who live far away virtually. The healthier the family relationships our sons have, the stronger and more secure they'll be when they need to bounce back from tough times.

Outside the Family

As our sons grow, they need to broaden their connections beyond their families. In the podcast interview with Blake Boles

I mentioned earlier in this book, he suggests that one way teens can find connections in the wider world is through summer camp and teen travel programs. This gives teens a safe place to test their autonomy and develop new relationships based on similar interests, as many camp and travel programs are themed. They can also join sporting teams, clubs, youth groups, acting troupes, bands and orchestras, and more. Look around your community to find things that might interest your sons.

In our northeast Ohio area, we found a program through Case Western Reserve University called Environmental Heroes. This program offers teens interested in science and the environment a chance to get involved in citizen science by learning about and studying the distribution of reptiles and amphibians in the local watersheds. Trevor has been in the program since his freshman year of high school and has made some wonderful friends and gained some unique experiences. What I've loved most about the program is that the teens run it themselves. An adult facilitator brings in guests and speakers, and scientists visit and teach the teens to use equipment, but for the most part, the teens are doing the advocacy work themselves.

By participating in programs like this and in summer camps or group activities, our sons learn that they have a place in the community beyond the four walls of their home. Connections like these show our sons that they're a valued part of a community they're active in and supported members of. They're safe. And when we help them find communities that support their passions and interests while promoting similar values to those we hold as families, our conversations with our boys are reinforced. They learn that mom and dad aren't the only ones who look for honesty, integrity, loyalty, and responsibility.

Don't discount the natural world either. As Richard Louv writes in *Last Child in the Woods: Saving Our Children from Nature Deficit Disorder*, "an indoor (or backseat) childhood does reduce some dangers to children; but other risks are heightened, including risks to physical and psychological health, risk to children's concept and perception of community, risk to self-confidence and the ability to discern true danger." Resilience is amplified when we are actively connected to nature. Many of our sons today are too busy to be connected to nature, and they're missing out on an important part of their sense of belonging. They need time to explore nature on their own.

Why discuss nature in a book about resilience, anyway? Louv goes on to say, "Passion is lifted from the earth itself by the muddy hands of the young; it travels along grass-stained sleeves to the heart. If we are going to save environmentalism and the environment, we must also save an endangered indicator species: the child in nature." Boys need to understand that they are part of the natural world; not just the human race. Nature gives them an even greater sense of belonging because they begin to see themselves as stewards of our planet's future. And, when our sons observe nature, they are met with an infinite number of examples of resilience, like the seasons bringing birth, maturity, death, and new birth again and again and again. Nature is an amazing teacher.

Nurture Meaningful Connections

When we're talking about resilience and emotional intelligence within the context of helping our sons make connections in the greater community and outside the walls of our home, we should be cautious. Caution is not synonymous with being a helicopter parent. It's not possible to love our children too much, but we do need to balance that natural instinct to protect them with our fear for their discomfort and the overprotection that results from our parental stress.

Years ago my family was part of a homeschool group that met weekly for field trips. It was perfect for us at the time, as I had a twelve-year-old, seven-year-old, five-year-old, and two-year-old. Regular classes in a co-op setting weren't going to be a good fit for us at that moment in our lives as I was too busy chasing after a toddler and a preschooler to teach classes, so pitching in wasn't going to work. This group was voluntary, and the information about where we'd be going along with costs associated were published in an email the month before so we could plan which of the meetups we wanted to attend.

At twelve, Trevor's asynchrony was very pronounced. He is an extremely bright and articulate kiddo–then and still–and his profound giftedness shows in discrepancies between his physical, academic, neurological, social, and emotional abilities. This means that while he could carry on a conversation with an adult at twelve like he was a colleague and discuss current events or other topics that required deep critical thinking, he was also often reprimanded for throwing mulch or pushing a kid out of the way instead of telling him that it was his turn (like a six-year-old might do). He'd talk like a much older child and act like a much younger child. While this is completely developmentally normal for a child with his identifications and diagnoses, it's not normal for most kids, so he tended to get in trouble at some point at these meetups and field trips every week.

Because he and his siblings have always had a flair for the dramatic, Trevor had invented a game called "Dramatic Deaths." Dramatic Deaths was played daily at our house and my heart would skip a beat occasionally with how realistically my then two-year-old son Isaac could fake "death by asphyxiation." They'd get up, rate each other's deaths, and try a new form. This game was a favorite, and neighbors would come, get out our bucket of foam swords, nerf guns, and martial arts training equipment, and they'd stage epic battles with many dramatic deaths in the backyard after school and on weekends. They'd borrow my phone and record each other, poring over footage and rating the drama. It was harmless, safe, and imaginative. It also was exactly what Peter Gray, PhD, defines as play in his writings at psychologytoday.com: an activity that is (1) self-chosen and self-directed; (2) motivated by means more than ends; (3) guided by mental rules; (4) includes a strong element of imagination; and (5) is conducted in an alert, active, but relatively non-stressed frame of mind. The kind of play, he stresses, that kids need to develop emotional intelligence, confidence, and problem-solving skills.

One playground meetup between organized field trips, my kids taught this game to the homeschool playgroup kids. Boys and girls alike whooped it up, chose sides, and brandished sticks as makeshift swords. They acted out historical battles and made up new ones of their own. I didn't think much about it because they were all safe, cognizant of each other, and careful not to actually hurt one another. They were happily engaged in free play filled with kids of multiple ages. For me, it was exactly what we hoped for in a peer group: other kids with a love of imaginative and active play, mixing along age groups, and getting along while looking out for one another.

It turned out that I was in the minority. The organizer of the group called me one evening after several weeks of the kids playing this game at playgrounds, in the fields of the apple orchard after apple picking, and in the backyards we rotated from time to time. She said that many of the mothers disliked battle games of any kind, and that they were growing increasingly uncomfortable with this particular battle game because their kids were becoming very convincing with their deaths, and they found that disturbing. I told her that I understood and that I'd ask Trevor, who was one of the oldest, to choose not to play it anymore when we met up with this group. He was disappointed, but agreed.

The problem, though, was that the other kids loved this active and imagination-filled game and begged him to play whenever he would show up at a gathering. He'd say *no*, then come over to me when they kept badgering him because he was the one who was yelled at every time someone pretended to die or fight. It was a lot of pressure to put on a twelve-year-old who just wanted to run and play wildly for a few hours while he had the opportunity to be surrounded by a bunch of other kids. It was hard for the other kids too, who reluctantly went back to swing on the swings or play tag. It was also difficult for me because it

Raising Resilient Sons

became clear that other moms in the group had very different and almost irreconcilable parenting styles than I did.

Children should be central to our lives, but it's very important that they are not the sole focus. Parenting groups serve two important purposes for parents of toddlers, preschoolers, and homeschoolers (and others–these groups are the main ones whose kids may not be in a group setting with other kids or who, themselves, might not be seeing other adults regularly). One is to allow kids the chance to be around other kids so they can be involved in peer groups and have opportunities for free play, which we talked about in Chapter Four. The other is for moms to have a chance to talk to other moms while their kids play to swap parenting advice, insight, and just talk adult to adult.

The pressure on all the kids, in this case, to stop playing a kid-created game they enjoyed eventually shut down the game for good, but it cast a light of suspicion on my twelve-year-old, the instigator of something foreign and mildly threatening to that particular group of moms. We stopped coming around to any of the free and open play meetups, attending only the more formal field trips and structured activities. The kids we knew outside that group, but who attended it as well, described the meetups as going back to a more benign existence with a focus on playground play and snack time. It was much safer play with less risk involved.

When our boys know that they're not only the center of their mother's world, but that she's constantly watching to see what they're saying or doing, how they're playing, and that they're doing things in a prescribed and scripted way, they begin to crack under the pressure. They feel the need to be perfect and worry excessively about letting parents down. They avoid taking risks or trying new things. For a while, when we still attended these free-play get-togethers after the banning of Dramatic Deaths, I noticed that Trevor wouldn't climb up the slide for fear of being yelled at for doing it the wrong way. He only played with the boys his age as that was what was expected of him, even though he got along much better with the older and the younger kids. His stress was palpable.

The fear of failing a parent or one of the other adults that are supposed to be looking out for them will prevent our sons from success because they'll struggle to develop the resilience to take the chances they need to take in order to overcome challenges. It just won't seem worth it to them.

Mothers need to create opportunities for their kids to experience connection and feel secure, but they need to step back, let kids have some freedom, and also nurture their own relationships with other adults so they can keep from burning out or overprotecting. When we do this and maintain deep relationships with our spouses, friends, colleagues, neighbors, or relatives, we model great examples of meaningful connections and relationships for our sons.

Like I encourage you to foster connection and a strong relationship with your sons, mama, I strongly encourage you to take care of yourself and your own relationships too. Cherish your children. Revel in your accomplishments. Nurture your relationships. Enjoy your favorite hobbies. If nothing else comes from any of this, you'll at least continually restore your energy so that you can bounce back more readily from hard times and the eventual "leaving the nest" to embrace the independent and successful adulthood all kids do at some point.

Nurturing and Letting Go

Let's think about this from the past to the future. Connection when our sons are little include snuggles, cuddles, cooing, and backpack carries. We count tiny fingers and toes. We rock little ones to sleep, kissing damp curls and running our fingertips over long eyelashes. But, as our sons grow older and hit milestone after milestone, we feel like we lose the connections we've worked so hard to establish.

But our sons need to show us they've grown, matured, and have tackled each new developmental challenge because when the time comes to let them go–to college, a new apartment, into marriage, trade school, or whatever–we need to know they're ready. Our boys spend their entire childhood needing us less and less. Think about the first visit to the zoo after your stroller-riding baby started walking. He didn't need you to carry him anymore. You lost that snuggly feeling of holding him up to see his favorite tigers in their exhibit. Now he climbs onto a rock and holds onto the fence to observe next to you instead of cuddled into you. Then, he's done, scrambling down the rock and off to another exhibit while you trail behind trying to keep up. This goes on and on, all the way through to young adulthood when they'll eventually tell us they don't need us to take care of them anymore.

As they move toward greater independence, our sons don't need us to protect them as much. They must break the connection to deal with their own stress as they take the next steps toward adolescence and beyond. Our sons are excited and look forward to each new step toward independence, but they're scared too. They may not be able to articulate it, but they worry about failing, losing us, or moving on to other friends. Sometimes they can't even imagine an adult life, so they're terrified they won't ever be independent.

And have you ever noticed that your son is moody, irritable, or regresses just before some new challenge is about to be met or milestone achieved? They seem to push us away when we think they might need us most. And they *do* need us more. Oftentimes our sons are pushing us away because it's easier than asking for help. Think about how much easier it is for your teenage son to say, "Mom, leave me alone. I don't need you to make a schedule for me like I'm a baby," than it is for him to say, "Gosh, Mom. Thank you. I really don't have any idea how to organize my freelance jobs, my class assignments, and manage my time playing with my friends online and with my new VR headset. I'd love to sit down with you or Dad to see how you'd tackle all these big jobs at once." It's so much easier to push back than it is to admit uncertainty when you're growing and trying to become who you are.

Years and years ago I read an article that likened parenting boys to parenting a lion cub. The analogy in the article was that sons are impulsive, wild, and love to explore and push boundaries, and as they grow this boundary pushing becomes more aggressive. They're most aggressive toward the people who are there to protect them. Instinctively they know that they'll still be loved and protected while they need it, so they try on their autonomy for size. Eventually they must strike out against the very people who loved them in order to find and create their own pride, or family. I like that this analogy reminds me to nurture while I can, let go when he needs me to, and comfort when he comes back to me, all preparing him to do the same when he nurtures his own family.

Our sons challenge us because they need to loosen the bonds of our connection that tells them (and us) that we have full responsibility for them. These challenges hurt us. They anger us. And this is all normal and predictable, even necessary. When we understand what is going on, we can respond, though, with compassion and empathy instead of fighting back to regain control. Each time we tighten the reins further, we risk being seen as unjust and sowing seeds of resentment. Instead, try to set appropriate rules and boundaries to give your sons a chance to gain independence while still being respectful of you and your parenting needs. Help them understand that you will push back and relax boundaries as he shows responsibility.

Balancing our need to know our boys are safe with their growing independence and need for separation is where it's tough for moms. We need to know that this process is, and should be, gradual, and that the job of children is to find their own identity, especially in adolescence. It's so tempting, though, to hold the bond too tightly or to fix things for our children.

In that same article from years ago, the author mused that he is often concerned when parents of tween and teen boys tell him they're not worried about what's going on in their child's life because their son tells them everything and that they're best friends. He goes on to say that it's critical that adolescents are working toward becoming individuals distinct and separate from their parents. That they're building on their parents' values and beliefs to think critically and form their own with those at the root. He explains that when boys go through this natural process, they see their parents as the stable rock they can use to measure others by, come back to when they need to feel grounded, or build off of.

The danger, he says, is that when parents worry too much about being a friend of their son's–dressing "cool," drinking with them, telling them everything they're thinking–that boys may be driven off a proverbial cliff of bad behavior as they try even harder to distance themselves from their parents. Our sons need us to be loving, connected, approachable, friendly, and even fun, but they don't need us to be their best friends. My son and I enjoy talking, watching shows together, drooling over new tech equipment, and hanging out together, but he also knows that I expect him to check in when he's with friends, be kind, and support his family.

Takeaways

▶ By widening the sphere of connection our sons have, we offer them the opportunity to be motivated by other good influences.

▶ As our sons grow, they need to broaden their connections beyond their families.

- When actively connected to nature, your sons amplify their resilience. Observing nature, they meet infinite examples of resilience, like the seasons bringing birth, maturity, death, and new birth again and again and again.

- The fear of failing you or another adult who's supposed to be looking out for them will prevent your sons from success because they'll struggle to develop the resilience to take the chances they need to take in order to overcome challenges.

- Foster connection and a strong relationship with your sons, but also take care of yourself and your own relationships too.

- Your sons may not be able to articulate it, but they worry about failing, losing us, and moving on to other friends. Sometimes they can't even imagine an adult life, so they're terrified they won't ever be independent.

- Remember to nurture while you can, let go when they need you to, and comfort when they come back to you, all preparing them to do the same when they nurture their own families.

- Your sons need you to be loving, connected, approachable, friendly, and even fun, but they don't need you to be their best friends.

Chapter Nine

Growing Strong Character

A child's character develops in accordance with the obstacles he has encountered...or the freedom favoring his development that he has enjoyed.

—Maria Montessori

Trevor came to me crying one evening when he was seven. It took a while, but I finally got him to start talking to me. He had been struggling for weeks with something that wasn't settling well, and he told me that it was making his tummy hurt, so he needed to talk about it. Worst-case scenarios galloped through my mind, and I started feeling butterflies in my own tummy. It turned out that he'd been feeling conflicted about a secret he was asked to keep.

We were scheduled to go on vacation to California for a few weeks, and one of the places we'd planned to visit was Legoland, where Trevor had decided he'd spend the money he'd been saving for months on a very large Lego set so that he could remember the visit every time he looked at it or played with it. He liked two sets, and he admitted that part of him was frustrated we wouldn't just buy both sets for him in the first place. Since it was important to my husband and me to help our children develop a healthy attitude about money and respect for possessions, we wanted him to choose one and earn the money to purchase it–which he did.

He broke down on the eve of our trip out to California because his grandmother had told him to buy one of the sets and that she'd just buy him the other one. She told him that she'd put it in her basement, where he could play with it when he came over, and after a few months, she'd have him bring it home with him and add it to his LEGO collection. By then, we'd never know because he already had so many sets anyway. He'd agreed with his grandma, was thrilled about it, really, because what little boy wouldn't want more LEGO sets rather than fewer? But knowing that we'd told him to choose one, that we wanted him to earn it, and that he'd have to lie to us about the entire plan kept eating at him.

He cried in my arms when he finished telling me and confessed that he felt so much better afterward. He said that he was sad because it meant I'd need to confront my mother about asking my son to lie to me while going against the boundaries we'd set up around the acquisition of possessions, and also because he knew that it meant he was only going to get one LEGO set after all.

Every family has different parameters for what good character means. Sometimes, as evidenced by this personal anecdote, the parameters may differ within an extended family. Some families may prioritize honestly and integrity over humility and respect, while others value individuality over generosity. Regardless, most families agree they don't want their kids to have certain character traits like hatred, dishonesty, bigotry, insensitivity, or selfishness. Most want their sons to grow up to be moral, responsible, kind, and honest. I do not have the right to tell you, though, which exact character traits to prioritize over others as you raise your own boys. I will say, though, that we all need to be active about developing the character of our sons.

Our sons hear so many opinions of who they should be, what they should look like, and how they should behave. Mixed messages abound and confuse even the best of kids. Character grows based on feedback and direction. Trevor knew that lying to us about getting another LEGO set would be wrong, and that even a lie by omission–or not saying anything, just hoping we wouldn't notice–wasn't right. His gut told him to come to us for help.

Mamas, we want to make sure to surround our kids with people who will reinforce the character traits we value and help them live up to the high moral standards we've set. We can't leave their character development to chance. And yes, I still advocate getting out of their way, letting them discover who they are, and encouraging them to play freely in mixed age groups, but we must be active participants in their character development. No doubt my mother thought she was helping her grandson get the things he wanted and was simply spoiling him a little. And if I wasn't such an active parent and hadn't built a relationship of trust and clear expectations, Trevor might have felt that it was better to lie and get all the toys he could ever want than deny himself that pleasure by letting me know what was up. Ultimately, in this situation, character won. He and I have had some great discussions over the last ten years since, about how even those closest to us can have different sets of values than we want to cultivate, and how it's important to always evaluate situations through our own morals and values before agreeing to anything that seems off.

Teaching Those Values

There are so many roadblocks to teaching our kids to be people of character. Society at large values many traits that seem incongruent with the idea of integrity, but we must fight those influences because strong character builds confidence, and confidence leads to the resilience and emotional awareness that we want to see in our sons. The culture at large values personal success, but we want to ensure that our sons aren't achieving outward shows of success through dishonesty. We want them to be hard working and to value kindness, empathy, compassion, and cooperation. We want them to know that winning is amazing but hollow if they don't play the game well. In fact, "how we play the game" is what defines us and shows our character.

So how do we do this? Telling our sons how to act, what to value, and how to care isn't enough. Telling them "be kind to your sister" or "help the neighbor out when you see her working in the yard" or "honesty is the most important value we hold" doesn't do enough. We have to show our sons what matters to us by what we teach, praise, and correct. We have to show them by living our values in every encounter, with whomever we meet up with. There are some simple and practical ways we can do this on a day-to-day basis.

Notice kindness often. It's easy to remember to praise our sons when they do something well or accomplish a task, but it's more important to remember to praise times when you see them acting in kindness, generosity, and thoughtfulness. Tell them you appreciate them and that you see the good they do. We also need to talk about the good we see in the world. It's easy to get caught up in the negative and talk about all the problems our culture faces when we're on the phone or with friends. But we need to remember that our sons are watching and listening. If we're only talking about the bad that's happening in our neighborhoods or in our country, then they'll get a skewed view of what it means to be an adult. Let them overhear you chat with a friend about how a mutual friend takes care of her aging mother. Or how the local church opened their doors to host meals in a time when unrest made eating at home unsafe. Or about how Dad used to go over and help his grandfather style his grandmother's hair each weekend. Share talk about everyday heroes in front of your sons and minimize the talk of scandals and conspiracies.

Treat others well. Your sons are watching you. When you go anywhere, they're observing you. Speak kindly to others, whether that's the cashier at the drive-through window, the librarian, your boss, or their friend's mother. They'll notice how you interact with other adults.

One of my now-adult cousins is an alcoholic. I remember being at family gatherings when I was young and watching the aunts and uncles–including his parents–sit around and visit, not really laughing or seeming to enjoy themselves until the beer and wine started circling more freely. Once the adults had begun drinking, they'd play cards and games and enjoy each other. I can't help but think that those observations early on in life contributed, among other things, to my cousin's choices and his struggle with alcohol and, eventually, drugs. Our kids watch and learn from how we adults interact and get along.

Encourage your sons to take responsibility for themselves and their choices. Resilient and emotionally intelligent boys acknowledge their successes and their failures. They take responsibility for their actions, and they work to improve themselves as a result of taking that responsibility. When they mess up, communicate the message that you still love them regardless and are proud of them when they take responsibility for their actions. If your sons learn to take responsibility for their choices, they'll understand cause and effect and that they are not entitled to what they haven't earned.

Encourage your sons to really think about the media they consume. Instead of telling them to "turn down that hateful music–it's trash," and risk pushing them further away, try asking them, "Have you really listened to the words he's singing? Do you hear how degrading that is to women? Maybe you should find other artists with a great band who have more uplifting and positive messages." Sit down and watch shows with them, and talk about what you're seeing. Take them to the movies. Characters in movies and television shows can be wonderful jumping-off points for conversations about character.

Build a Better World

Your sons should know that small contributions, one small act at a time, can make the world better. Model this for them by being aware of need around you. Pick up the trash in the park. Hold a door for a mom with a stroller. Carry an elderly person's bags to her car for her. Make time to talk to your children about the injustices in the world. Make giving to charities an everyday part of your family culture by choosing a new cause each week or month. Amounts aren't as important as actions because every little bit does help, and just by having your children involved in choosing the cause, you're setting up a future of givers. When you talk to your sons about giving, explain that it's not *just because it feels good*; it's because it's right and helps others.

Honor differences. We live in a nation whose strength is in its diversity. We may feel connected to familiar groups related to our own ethnicity, race, political beliefs, religion, or socioeconomic status, and want our sons to feel that link with others who share their values. This natural desire for connection to others like us should never be an excuse for not teaching our sons tolerance, though. It's important to avoid teaching them any kind of prejudice or to think of people who don't belong to the same groups we do as *other*. Honoring differences means respecting the fact that different groups also have very strong values. Stay open to having rich discussions with and learning from these different groups.

Prejudice isn't always intentional, malicious, or even conscious. It's based on limited information and comes in many forms, all with negative consequences. At the very least, prejudice prevents us from getting to know one another for who we truly are. Recently my sons and I have been discussing racism, though we've talked about it in the past and will continue talking about it in the future. I asked my youngest son what the word meant to him. He said, "It's when you don't like someone because they have black or brown skin. It makes me sad because Carlos, Carson, Nick, and Briana have brown skin, and they're my friends. A racist person wouldn't like them and they're too nice not to like."

Our country is incredibly diverse, and the entire world is more and more connected every day. Our sons need to be raised free from prejudice so that they can thrive in a connected world. Not matter how subtly prejudice surfaces, even our littlest kiddos can pick up on these building blocks of racism. They're sponges and absorb ideas and attitudes from everyone around them. We can't overlook outside influences like media, books, friends, music, and other family members. Search out diverse children's books, watch movies with characters of different races and ethnicities, and listen to music from a variety of cultures. Help them look for bias in their media as they grow older. Ask: Who are the heroes and heroines? Who are the smart and capable characters? Who is bumbling and making mistakes? Who are the villains? Who are the criminals? Who solves the problems? Who leads? Who follows?

It wouldn't be honest to ignore that minorities are portrayed more often in unflattering or unrealistic ways. Our sons will live up to or down to our expectations of them. If you are raising Black, Latino, Asian, Indigenous, or other minority sons, point out these distorted messages. Talk with pride about your heritage, background, ancestors, and stories. If you are raising White sons, point out the unfairness and dishonesty of these messages. Talk about how some minorities rarely appear in media, and when they do, they are cast as stereotypes. Don't just tell your sons that these messages and stereotypes are untrue, show them by sharing positive stories and images of diverse groups. Multicultural books, music, toys, artifacts, and museum visits can help our boys understand and appreciate the history and culture of all people.

There are so many character-building lessons to teach and conversations to have with our sons around these topics that it could take an entire book, and I'll admit that this small section doesn't do the issue justice. But I feel committed not only to acknowledge the importance of tolerance, but of continuing the conversation and learning alongside our sons.

When our sons are raised with strong characters, they have a core set of values to return to when times get tough. And they will get tough. This makes them resilient in the most trying of times. Children raised with character also help build a society where people treat each other with integrity, honesty, and fairness.

Self-Control

Boys who are honest, show integrity, and are fair easily build on those characteristics and can demonstrate self-control. You've heard about the Stanford marshmallow experiment published in 1972, that studied delayed gratification, haven't you? Let's revisit the study. In the 1960s, Walther Mischel, a Stanford professor, began a series of psychological experiments where he tested hundreds of children between the ages of four and five years old. The experiments were simple. A child was brought into a room, and the researcher put a marshmallow in front of the child. The researcher then explained that he needed to leave the room, and if the marshmallow was still there when he got back, he'd reward the child with a second marshmallow. If the marshmallow was gone, then the child would only get that one. One treat now or two treats later.

The study became famous not because of the often-entertaining footage of the kids trying to resist temptation, but because of the information that emerged many years later. Researchers followed up with the kids and tracked their progress in many areas as they grew. And the results were clear. The kids who were willing to delay gratification and wait on the second marshmallow had higher test scores, lower levels of substance abuse and obesity, better social skills, and a better response to stress. As researchers continued to follow the kids over the course of forty years, the results bore out again and again as the group that delayed gratification continued to succeed.

Resilient adults can delay gratification. They can delay buying treats so that they can eat healthier. They can delay watching television so they can complete work projects. So many things that feel good to us in the moment can get in the way of our ultimate success.

It's not easy to get kids to delay gratification. They naturally want things the moment they think of it, but we can work to help them learn this critical skill. Mamas, we're committed to raising resilient sons, and helping them learn to delay gratification is the cornerstone to them learning self-control. Remember, though, that this skill can take years to learn and to hone. You would set your sons up for failure if you expected them to control their impulses at all times. It's just not possible.

My teen worked on freelance projects for months, saving every penny to buy himself that VR headset I mentioned earlier. Everyone in the family has played on it with him except me. I've been working on this book for weeks and as it's been harder for me to write during a pandemic than I expected it to be, I told him that while I really want to play with him, it will have to wait until I've completed the book and sent it in to my editor. He's cajoled, begged, and gotten frustrated with me, and I've held strong because the truth is that I'd love to walk away from my computer and play with him. I already make a point to play other video games and watch shows with him, but I also want him to see me choosing to delay gratification and reward myself later. One of the reasons I've chosen to write and speak as a career is so that I have more time to spend with my kids, and I'm easily persuaded to do things with them and put off my work. I'm staying strong this time, though.

Usually, when I work on a project like a book, I leave the house for a few hours each day and work in a coffee shop or at the library. All of the options I usually use are closed down, so I'm writing this amidst constant interruption and chaos. If I took the time right now to go up to my teen's attic room and strap on that VR headset, I'd get caught up in a make-believe world, a shared experience with him, and I'd have trouble regrouping and getting work done right now. Because he really wants me to play but also understands the need for self-control in situations like this, he's been cheering me on, holding me accountable for a daily word count, and taking his younger siblings swimming when they're bored so I can keep working. He said to me just tonight, "Mom, I'm proud of your hard work, but I'll be glad when you hit send on the manuscript. Can we play all day together?"

Children and teens who are able to make wise choices and show self-control learn that they can trust their ability to take charge of their own lives. They aren't afraid to take the risks resilient people need to take to overcome adversity. They aren't afraid to fail. They learn from mistakes and don't repeat negative patterns of behavior.

Takeaways

▶ Value responsibility, kindness, and honesty in your sons.

▶ Be active about developing the character of your sons.

- Make sure to surround your kids with people who will reinforce the character traits you value and help them live up to the high moral standards you've set.

- Strong character builds confidence, and confidence leads to the resilience and emotional awareness that you want to see in your sons.

- Show your sons what matters to you by what you teach, praise, and correct. You have to show them by living your values in every encounter with whomever you meet up with.

- Notice kindness often.

- Treat people well.

- Encourage your sons to take responsibility for themselves and their choices.

- Teach your sons that small contributions can make the world better–one small act at a time.

- Honoring differences means respecting the fact that different groups also have very strong values and staying open to having rich discussions with and learning from them.

- Children and teens who are able to make wise choices and show self-control learn that they can trust their ability to take charge of their own lives.

Part Four

Nurturing Determination

You gain strength, courage, and confidence by every experience in which you really stop to look fear in the face. You are able to say to yourself, "I have lived through this horror. I can take the next thing that comes along."

—Eleanor Roosevelt

Perseverance is grit-tough resourcefulness that remains after everything else has been stripped away. Grit is the determined drive that fuels the knowledge and belief that you can make things happen, and you are not a passive bystander in your own life. With grit, you are an active influence.

This is what we want our sons to know in order to continue to grow their strength, resiliency, and emotional intelligence throughout their lives. It's easy for our sons to feel they are passive receivers of the things that happen rather than active doers So many things are out of their control when they're young, it's easy for them to be worn down by everyone telling them what they need to do. To help them grow in their determinations, though, we need to help them understand that they have control over their lives.

In the book *The Self-Driven Child: The Science and Sense of Giving Your Kids More Control Over Their Lives*, Ned Johnson and William Stixrud describe "locus of control" as a person's belief about whether what happens as a result of their behaviors are dependent on what they choose to do or outside factors altogether. For example, a child with an external locus of control who fails his test would say it's because the teacher didn't tell him what was going to be on the test. A child with an internal locus of control who fails that same test would say it was because he didn't study hard enough.

Having a strong internal locus of control leads to greater success, taking responsibility, and bouncing back when things go wrong, then trying again and doing things better than ever. Mama, we can help our kids develop a strong internal locus of control by doing a few simple things.

- ▶ We can encourage them to take responsibility for both their failures and their successes.

- ▶ We can remind them that it is okay to be imperfect.

- ▶ We can remind them of some of their past successes to encourage them to show grit and persevere.

- ▶ Most importantly, we can remember that once they start seeing that connection between effort and success, they'll keep trying.

Do the hard work with them, mama, and help them really be mindful of what they are truly capable of.

Chapter Ten

Mindful Living

Mindfulness is simply being aware of what is happening right now without wishing it were different; enjoying the pleasant without holding on when it changes (which it will); being with the unpleasant without fearing it will always be this way (which it won't).

—James Baraz

Shawna's oldest son was often the target of bullies in elementary school. She worked extensively with him to help him know his own worth and be calm in the moment when issues would occur. He worked with therapists and at home to be mindful–aware of his body and mind in all situations–and to be fully present in every moment. Ultimately, they made the decision to homeschool, pulling him out of the system that was not meeting his needs.

Long after she had begun homeschooling her son, she ran into another mom who had also had a child in her son's former class. This mom hugged Shawna immediately and told her that she had never gotten to share a story about her boy. Shawna's son had stood up for hers with the class bully. The mom told Shawna that her son had turned to hers and said, "You are not the problem here. He is. Next time he's mean to you, you remember that." For so long, Shawna had worried about the long-term impact those bullies might have had in her son's life. She wasn't worried anymore.

The difficult thing for boys–all children, really–is staying mindful and in the moment. Being mindful is when you stay present in the moment *as it is*. You do not daydream or give in to distraction. It's pretty easy to encourage our sons (and ourselves) to be mindful when sitting on a cozy chair, soft music playing. Or to focus on the moment for a breath or two. But learning to do so is proven to lower stress, protect heath, lift moods, and help our sons be more aware of themselves, their feelings, and their body's reactions to their environment.

We talked earlier in the book about neuroplasticity, and this is where we can really leverage it for the good of our boys, mama. Our sons' nervous systems are created to be adaptable and changed by their experiences. It's why we want to flood their childhood with so much good, nurture them, and build connections with people who will help them thrive. To effectively convert passing experiences into lasting strengths, our sons need to be able to focus their attention on experiences long enough to concentrate the effects into their nervous systems. Like Shawna's son, we want ours to be able to remember and use their past experiences to do good. To be mindful of what others might be feeling. Unfortunately, so many of our sons struggle to focus. Their minds dart this way and that. We live in a media-drenched, multitasking, shiny-object-chasing, stress-filled, anxiety-riddled, depressive culture that can render it nearly impossible for the best of us to focus, and some of us are just naturally more distractible than others.

While writing this book, I learned about a new app called Self Control designed for a Mac computer. It blacklists popular URLs like those for social media, news sources, comedy sites, and streaming services. The user can also put in sites of their own choosing to block out. Once they set a timer for the blackout, those sites are unreachable–even if they were to delete the app from their computer–until the time set is complete. I told my teen about this app because he is working on freelance audio and video editing projects while getting ready to start a college class and an internship program that will be paying for the majority of his degree, and he, like me, is naturally distractible. He's already used it twice, declaring it the best app ever invented.

With mindfulness, your sons can regulate their attention to get the most out of beneficial situations while limiting the influence of harmful ones. Sometimes willpower works, or writing lists, or using other behavioral techniques. Sometimes our boys may need the help of an app like mine to help train themselves to be more mindful. The best part of all of this, though, is that mindfulness can be strengthened. It's kind of like a mental muscle, and your sons can strengthen it by making it a part of their everyday lives. Over time, this continuity will empower them with a sustained presence of mind that is grounded and unwavering.

What's the Point?

So how can you help your sons weave mindfulness into their days without making too big a deal of it, and why should you even bother in the first place? Well, your son's attention is *his*. He owns it, and the sooner you teach him to keep it sacred, not allowing the rushing world to take it from him against his will, the better. Model slowing down and doing only one thing at a time with your full attention. When he grows up seeing you fully focused and in the moment, he learns to do that too, and that will carry over to his own relationships and jobs.

Start simple by playing mindfulness games with your sons, reading books with them, and setting timers to focus on your breathing together. In a deck of cards I wrote entitled *The Anxiety Toolkit*, an entire section details easy and fun mindfulness activities you can do with your children to help them learn to slow down and appreciate their world.

Finding Their Safe Place

Mindfulness allows your boys to begin to truly know themselves and go deep into what makes them tick. If you've done an active job of building a strong connection with your sons, they'll open up to you, deepening your relationship. Sometimes, though, as they begin deepening their understanding of their feelings and themselves, your sons may feel uncomfortable. A safe space is somewhere they can retreat to as they think through big thoughts. Helping them to create one is a healthy way to encourage them to do the hard work of knowing themselves.

For young kids, this safe space can be as simple as a tent in their room, piled high with pillows and fleece and stocked with books, lights, and a music or audio book player. As they grow, give them some say in designing their rooms, if possible. My teen just decorated his new room when we moved. He is in the attic room, double the size of any other room in the house, like his own studio apartment. One side is where his bed, desk, and an old futon sit. The other side is a studio for video and photo work. He spends a lot of his time up there now, working, playing, thinking about his future. It's the best of all worlds for him right now: a retreat where he can think deep thoughts and be alone, and a quick two flights of stairs to descend into the hustle and bustle of activity where his younger siblings play.

Being Happy, Effective, Loving, and Wise

Therapists agree on three main ways for engaging the mind. First, you can teach your sons to explore all aspects of what's going on around them in the moment with all of their senses, thoughts, and emotions. They can feel their feelings. They can experience the experience. What's going on in the moment may change, but they shouldn't do anything active to change it. They should just be there.

Second, you can teach your sons to minimize the negative in a given situation. They can decrease the pain and harm by preventing it, reducing it, or stopping it altogether. Some of the ways they can do this is by venting to you, writing in a journal, drawing a picture, walking away from the situation, stopping themselves from a cycle of negative thoughts, or ease their own tension with deep breathing or relaxing their bodies.

Finally, they can learn to increase the positives in a situation. Help them focus on whatever is enjoyable by creating it. They can remember and draw from beneficial experiences when they need an influx of those positive feelings. They could breathe in to improve blood flow and energy, remember a fun time they had, be realistic about the impact a situation will actually have on their life, or motivate themselves by imagining a positive outcome.

Your sons can get great at coping, healing, and fostering their own well-being–with your help. Mindfulness is integral to this since they can't cope, heal, or be grounded without it. The best thing, though, about practicing mindfulness is that it will help your sons grow the inner resources that lead to greater resilience and emotional intelligence innately. For example, focusing on the positive and increasing its effect in their life grows self-compassion in your sons, giving them more resources to combat painful feelings.

Wants and Needs

Help your sons think about their experience when it comes to expressing their wants and needs. Encourage them to notice how they are affected by the rest of the family's response to those wants and needs. Talk to them about what they notice. If people are kind and loving, they probably feel supported and good about themselves. However, if they're dismissive, they may feel as if their needs don't matter or that their wants are embarrassing. They may begin to feel like there is something wrong with them.

The residual effects of these interactions are stored within the somatic nervous system, to form an internal awareness that allows a person to reach their full potential because they are not only attuned to the physicality of what happens to them, but also their inner reactions to experiences. How we respond to our sons' wants and needs from the time they're tiny directly affects how they view the things they feel they need throughout their lives, such as which wants and needs are allowed, which should be hidden, and which are shameful. Ask yourself:

▶ How do I respond to my sons' wants?

▶ How do I support my sons' needs and wants?

▶ Are there any changes I should make in how I respond to my sons' wants and needs?

Being mindful in this way can help us mamas remember to nurture and support our sons in ways that empower and help them understand, rather than control and change them. After all, their thoughts, dreams, wishes, wants, needs, and desires are all real and valid. They just might not be appropriate or realistic in certain situations. It's up to us to support them while teaching them natural boundaries in ways that won't undermine their growth or shame them, damaging our relationship.

Three Basic Emotional Needs

All human beings have three basic emotional needs that ground them and help them stay balanced and sure of themselves. Let's take a look at these needs from the perspective of raising resilient sons.

First, our boys need to feel safe. This include knowing that they'll have access to all that will keep them alive and healthy, and also that they won't be attacked if they speak out or express themselves. Second, they need to be satisfied. This feeling can result from simple things like feeling full after a good meal, reading a great book, or spending time with a great friend, and also more abstract things like believing life is worth living, working toward (and achieving) a big goal, and being recognized for their accomplishments. Finally, above all, our sons need connection. Like we talked about in the last chapter, they need to feel worthy and loved. They take care of their need for connection by attaching to good people in their lives, as demonstrated when your little guy comes up behind you and rubs your back or your older son texts a friend just to say hello. We can make sure our boys feel connected by giving them time–with us when they're younger and with friends as they grow.

Owning Needs

In a culture that expects boys to "man up," "be a man," or "just do it," it might be embarrassing for our boys to admit that they have needs. It's up to us to remind them that we all depend on others, and admitting it is a sign of growth and maturity. True manhood is being brave enough to admit and own normal neediness. Being a healthy person doesn't come from denying needs, it comes from being mindful of one's needs as well as the needs of others.

Help your sons stay mindful of their needs throughout the day. They might feel unsafe. If so, assure them of their safety when they feel uneasy, irritable, or stressed. If they're feeling bored, frustrated, or lost, they may be missing out on satisfaction and need to look for ways to feel fulfilled. When they're feeling hurt, envious, resentful, or down on themselves, they may be crying out for connection of some kind. My seven–year-old just said to me today, "Mommy, when will your book be done? Um... sorry. I know it will be a good book and all, but I just want to go swimming with you." The reality is that I have been working a lot more than I normally do because I have my regular work, family, and homeschool responsibilities; am taking a very intense course to help me with some technical aspects on a project for work; and am researching and writing this book. This leaves little margin time for swimming, though it's only for a time period of less than two months. To my little boy who needs connection, it seems like forever. (And was anyone else melted by the way he assured me what I'm writing would be good? I just love little boys...)

When our sons are brave enough to reach out and let their needs be known, we need to validate them and try to help them meet their needs so they keep being brave. I can't swim today, even though I'd love to give into my son's needs and wants. I have a babysitter here and need to use the time to get several thousand words written as well as record two scheduled interviews for my podcast. Since it's the only day my babysitter is available, I need to work now so that I can put my computer away for the weekend and really focus on my family then. It's our job, mamas, to respond and reassure in situations like this. I gave him a quick hug in this case–a "squeezy hug," where I hug him tight–and told him that I'd tuck him in at bedtime and he should go enjoy the time he has with his babysitter, whom he loves.

Being Grateful

Fostering an environment filled with positive emotions like gratefulness is a key component of raising resilient sons. From a practical standpoint, these feelings strengthen the body's response to stress, strengthen its immune system, and support physical health. They help us dig out of despair after loss or trauma. They help us see the big picture and often-missed opportunities. They encourage perseverance. They connect people.

Try this: ask your sons to think of a time they felt thankful. Maybe it was while eating their favorite dessert or playing with a friend. Then, ask them what they feel when they think of it. If it helps, you can model this by talking about a time you were grateful. There's a feeling that comes when we reflect on a time we were grateful. It's a sense of calm, needs being met, satisfaction, and meaningfulness. Thankfulness just feels good. It grows optimism, happiness, self-worth, compassion, generosity, forgiveness, and resilience. It also combats against envy, depression, stress, loneliness, and sleeplessness.

Gratitude isn't about denying trouble or injustice. It's about appreciating what is. It's about noticing the flowers that bloom in your yard, bringing color from early spring throughout late summer. It's the way your baby boy giggles and reaches for you to comfort him when he falls. It's your teen calling you at midnight to ask if he can stay the night at your nephew's house because they're having fun hearing stories about you, your husband, and your brother- and sister-in-law from before they were born. There are things to be grateful for every moment of every day if we can train ourselves and our sons to look for them.

When your family experiences pain, help them look for the gifts that go along with it. For example, we lost my father-in-law this past fall. He'd been very ill and declining for a long time. We finally convinced him to move in with us so we could care for him. We bought a bigger house far closer to family than the one we had lived in for the last decade that was an hour away. Our new home had a room for him and was very near his other children, his sisters, and his nieces and nephews. Just as we made our final plans to pick up our keys and prepare his room, he passed suddenly at the care facility he was staying at. We got those keys on the day we buried him.

It was an incredibly difficult time for the kids, particularly my oldest son, who was very close with his grandfather. Over the next few weeks we moved and learned about our new area, appreciating things we hadn't given much thought to before. There was a deck to go out and enjoy our morning coffee on while watching the birds my father-in-law loved so much. Most of all we were all thankful to be close to family for the first time since my husband and I were married. My kids have spent more time with their cousins, aunts, and uncles in the last few months than they have their entire lives. And my teen, who still misses his grandfather terribly, is so grateful that his closest friend now is my nephew. Liam and Trevor are less than a year apart and have never had the chance to hang out. They spend at least several days a week together now that we live fifteen minutes from them. Good comes from bad if we watch for it and appreciate it.

Try to make gratitude a regular part of your sons' day. You could make it a practice to go around the dinner table and have each family member say three things they're grateful for, or do this at bedtime. If he's a kiddo who likes writing, have him keep a gratitude journal like I mentioned in Chapter One. Try sitting down with your sons, each of you writing a thank you letter to someone just to let them know they've made an impact on your lives.

Embracing Calm

Building family rituals around gratitude–like the dinnertime exchange mentioned above–can help your sons stay grounded in their belief in themselves and feel sure of their own capabilities. Everyone faces challenges, but that calm sense of self that comes from being grounded can see your boys through tough times and challenges. Calm comes easily when we're relaxed and happy, but it's a little harder to harness when we're under duress. Naturally, this is when we need calm the most. When the bases are loaded and the winning run is on third, a batter needs to be calm, focused, and alert in order to connect with the ball to drive their teammate in for the win.

Fear, paralysis, doubt, and retreat come in when threats seem bigger to our sons than their ability to handle them. Sometimes this is actually true, like when our teen has procrastinated to the point that there is absolutely no way he can meet a deadline or turn in an assignment on time. But more often threats look bigger than they actually are while internal resources seem much smaller than they are. Recently my teen asked if he could talk with me about his future. He had been thinking and had come to the conclusion that not only was he unprepared for adulthood, but he wouldn't ever be able to earn a living, pay bills, keep a house of his own, or have a lasting relationship with anyone.

The exercise I took him through is one you can use with your little guys as well as your adult sons if they need your support in a situation that seems too big for them to ever handle.

1. **Ask your son to describe his thoughts and fears.** I invited my teen to tell me everything that was on his mind in as much detail as he could. I listened without interjection or advice. I did ask him to be more specific at times, though. Instead of "I'll never be able to have a house," I asked him to clarify the reasoning to "I spend my money as soon as I get it, so I'll never be able to hold onto the money I earn to pay for all the things that go into having a house." That's concrete and something we can tackle together.

2. **Ask him how likely each scenario is.** In the example of my teen, would he be forever without a job that could sustain him? That one, we agreed, is pretty unlikely as he already runs a business, is about to start an internship while he earns his degree in computer science, and the last time we were in the Apple store together, the manager was so impressed with his knowledge he offered him a job on the spot and was disappointed to find out he was only seventeen, a year below the minimum age to work there. Most of the time we're worried, it's about something that might happen, so it helps to talk through the actual possibility.

3. **Finally, talk through each of those and decide how bad each would really be.** We focused on what he'd experience if his fears came to pass. How badly would he actually feel, and for how long? His favorite uncle is fifty years old and has never been married. He throws amazing holiday parties for all ages, goes around to the nieces' and nephews' houses on the evening before Saint Nicholas Day and fills their shoes with candy and oranges, is a physician with a thriving medical practice, has regular game nights for any and all who are free, and takes his widowed mother on bucket-list trips around the world each year. There's a good chance, once you help your sons think deeper about their fears, that they'll realize they wouldn't feel too badly for too long.

When you're going through this exercise with your sons, help them think about times when they've drawn on their inner confidence, grit, compassion, perseverance, and other strengths to handle issues that have come up in their lives. Ask them how they could tap into those same inner resources to deal with the current challenge they're facing.

Takeaways

▶ Mindfulness can lower stress, protect heath, lift moods, and help your sons be more aware of themselves, their feelings, and their body's reactions to their environment.

▶ Mindfulness is when your sons can regulate their attention to get the most out of beneficial situations while limiting the influence of harmful ones.

▶ The sooner you teach your sons to keep their attention sacred rather than letting the rushing world take it from them against their will, the better.

▶ You can teach your sons to be with whatever is there in the moment.

▶ You can teach your sons to minimize the negative in a given situation.

▶ You can teach them to increase the positives in a situation.

▶ How you respond to your sons' wants and needs from the time they're tiny directly affects how they view the things they feel they need throughout their lives.

▶ Your sons need to feel safe, satisfied, worthy, and loved.

▶ Being a healthy person doesn't come from denying needs, it comes from being mindful of one's needs as well as the needs of others.

▶ When your sons are brave enough to reach out and let their needs be known, you need to validate them and try to help them meet their needs so they keep being brave.

▶ Good comes from bad if you watch for it and appreciate it.

▶ Often, threats look bigger than they actually are, while internal resources seem much smaller than they are.

Chapter Eleven

When Resilience Is Hard

The friend in my adversity I shall always cherish most. I can better trust those who helped to relieve the gloom of my dark hours than those who are so ready to enjoy with me the sunshine of my prosperity.

—Ulysses S. Grant

Isaiah was placed with Aurie and her husband as a foster child at fourteen days old. He was born addicted to crack cocaine and had seven additional substances in his bloodstream at birth. Aurie, her husband, and her girls were no strangers to difficult foster situations as they'd fostered high-risk and addicted babies before, along with other children born with severe special needs, and have since adopted three children out of foster care.

When he arrived at their home, he was a four-pound baby boy who cried all the time. His nervous system was always on overdrive and he could barely handle his everyday existence. He didn't tolerate being held, rocked, or fed. It was a constant struggle to figure out what he was trying to tell her as Aurie worked tirelessly with him to help him overcome addiction and get on a track that could help him live a happy and safe life.

When Isaiah was six months old, he was referred to a developmental pediatrician, who told Aurie that he would struggle his whole life. He told her that Isaiah would have many limitations with cognitive, receptive, and expressive language. He would likely have major behavioral issues, and it would be extremely difficult for him to understand and communicate. This was devastating for Aurie to hear, but she and her husband were determined that, no matter how long they had with him in their home, they would make sure he had the absolute best possible start they could give him.

They enrolled him in an early intervention program and worked with him and multiple therapists day after day after day. His therapies included simple movements and sensory play to help him learn to regulate his system, as well as language therapy that focused on simple phrases and expressions.

Despite the predictions of the pediatrician as well as the expectations of numerous other doctors and therapists, Isaiah improved every day. He spoke his first word at twelve months old and completely took off after that. Now, two years later, this beautiful boy—adopted into this family at two-and-a-half–can use both expressive and receptive language. He uses reasoning skills and shows empathy daily. The little guy who "would never talk" is a complete chatterbox, to the delight of his four siblings, and rattles off compound and complex sentences with ease, using advanced vocabulary for his age. Aurie and her husband tell their kids that they can do anything, and Isaiah proves it to his siblings and himself every day.

Children who know that they can control their environment and influence what happens to them hold a powerful key to hanging on to the resilience you've worked so hard to build in them along the way. It's equally important, though, for them to have a keen understanding of the things they can't control, as there's nothing worse than wasting time and energy on something they can never impact or change, using up all the inner resources they've built up to draw from when they can make an impact.

Remember that your job is to guide your sons as they figure out how to navigate what they can and can't control, so they can regulate their own reactions as a result. When we practice our empathetic listening skills often with our sons, they'll naturally come to us more often when they're struggling, and it will be very tempting to jump in and solve problems for them. After all, we really do want what's best for our boys. Even if we can fix things for them, though, we shouldn't. Instead, we should guide them through the process of coming up with their own solutions. They'll usually get there on their own if you facilitate the problem solving with open-ended questions. And, if they get to the end of the process and there's no real solution available to them, that's the time to give them a big hug and remind them that sometimes things are out of our control, but you'll always be there for them.

When Times Are Tough

We can do everything in our power, mamas, to help our boys develop resilience, but sometimes extreme challenges come along that test even the most resilient among us. When we know in advance that tough times are coming, like the impending death of a beloved grandparent, moving away from the best friend your son has known his entire life, or a divorce, we can work to prepare our sons. In times of sudden or unexpected crisis, however, as much as we'd like to get our sons ready to face what's happening, we're caught up in it too and are working to be resilient ourselves.

This is why we need to strengthen our sons' emotional intelligence and help them to develop resiliency all the time. This should be an ongoing aspect of your parenting–almost like preventative medicine–a routine that builds up your sons' inner resources and stores it for those unimaginable times.

In tough times your boys will be looking to you, so it's important you keep your own inner resources shored up as well. You need to model stability and self-care while letting your kids and teens know that they're safe. The effect events like tornadoes, hurricanes, earthquakes, terrorist attacks, and war have on kids has given us some understanding of how we can be prepared to respond to crises in ways that empower our sons to be resilient while still nurturing them and being their safety net.

One of the most important things you can do in extreme times is to listen to your children. It's a very simple but effective way for you to show your sons you love them and accept their feelings while they're puzzling their way through things. As I mentioned earlier, when the country shut down for the COVID-19 pandemic in March 2020, I was in Texas with my teen son Trevor. I was speaking at a homeschooling convention, and he was managing the booth I share with another speaker, my friend Pam Barnhill. The convention was supposed to run through Saturday night, but the city made the decision to shut down the convention on Friday afternoon.

After the announcement was broadcast over the speaker system, a kind of frenzy of movement followed. Vendors, speakers, and attendees all worked quickly to make the most of the last two hours they had in the exhibit hall. Parents purchased too much curriculum and fun games and supplemental resources for their homeschools, vendors and speakers tried frantically to rebook their flights for an earlier departure, and we all tried to pack up quickly. Unfortunately, Pam, Trevor, and I were stuck with our original departure for early Sunday morning, as we'd rented furniture to have in our booth so weary homeschool moms could come, sit, and chat about all things homeschooling and parenting, and the rental agency couldn't retrieve the furniture until Saturday morning.

The area near the convention center had been busy and bustling since Wednesday night, when Trevor and I had flown in. Thousands of people had been milling around, restaurants overflowed with lines, and families congregated on every corner. On Saturday morning, when we walked from the hotel to the rental agency and then back to the hotel, it was eerie. In less than twelve hours, the place was completely deserted. We saw one person on our walk over to the convention center and three or four on the way back to the hotel. It didn't feel threatening, but because it was so off, it didn't feel safe either.

That afternoon, since we were stuck at the hotel with nowhere to go, Trevor opted to hang out in our room alone watching movies and finishing off the snacks we'd bought in our grocery order, while I went upstairs to Pam's room to work and visit for a bit. Later that evening, Trevor was very quiet, and I asked if he wanted to talk about what was on his mind. He did. He talked and talked and talked. Things had been swirling through his head all day. Would we make it home? Would the planes be grounded? If the city could shut down convention centers and our state could shut down schools, what would stop them from shutting down planes and state borders? What would happen if we had to quarantine here at the hotel because we weren't allowed out of Texas? The sudden shutdown was traumatic, the trauma compounded by the fact that we were far from home, causing all sorts of inner turmoil. Frankly, his questions were valid but I just couldn't answer them. I had no idea in that moment, as things changed every time I turned on the news.

In times of crisis, listening helps us become detectives. We can look for clues to figure out what our kids are really struggling with, what they've heard, what they understand, what they don't understand, how they are interpreting what's going on, and what kind of help they need from us. When we listen to our sons during a crisis, we should listen for to clear up misunderstandings in particular so that they're not actually making a situation more frightening than it needs to be.

Younger boys may not be able to tell you exactly what is going on inside their heads when you ask them, so listening might look different. Your sons may need help to find the words to talk about their feelings. Try sitting with them while they play or draw, and ask them to act out or draw what's going on in their minds. Model for them by telling them what you're feeling or what you think they might be feeling. Encourage them to show their feelings in creative ways.

Older tweens and teens might put on a figurative mask by talking to you in terms of other people. "Liam has been sleeping with his shoes on because he wants to be able to run right outside if a big aftershock hits. Isn't he crazy?" Help your son keep his figurative mask on by continuing to talk about fears in relation to other people, even if you suspect he's really the one who is frightened. You can say something like, "I can understand where Liam's coming from. Being woken up by an earthquake as strong as yesterday's was, then feeling several aftershocks throughout the day can be unsettling. What do you think Liam should do to help himself feel safer?" Encourage your older kids to share feelings. Ask questions and make sure you don't minimize or belittle them in any way. Be calm and age appropriate in all of your answers.

Don't force your child to talk, though. Some kids are deeply affected by crises, but act like they aren't. They retreat instead, keeping quiet. These kiddos may do better with a more normal routine. My youngest, during the months and months of lockdowns for the coronavirus pandemic, had seemed completely unaffected, almost thriving, while stuck at home with all outside activities cancelled. One day he shouted out, "I don't know what's wrong with me, but I just want to see someone besides my family and go somewhere beside my house," and then he cried in my arms.

There's no need to push kids to talk before they're ready, especially if you're clear that you're there for them and have shown them you're empathetic and a safe space for them in the past. You can model taking comfort by talking things out with others. Let them see you talking to your older kids, on the phone with a friend, or to your spouse. Talk out loud about how much better you feel now that you've talked it out.

When a crisis such as an act of terror, a natural disaster, riots, or a pandemic is happening, it's very important to communicate directly with your sons so they understand what's going on and what you are doing as a family to stay safe and healthy. Gather everyone together and get in a comfortable spot. Doing so increases feelings of security. If your kids are younger, give them only enough detail and information to feel safe. If you have older kids, go into more depth, and make sure they have an opportunity to share their thoughts. If your kids range in ages, pull everyone together first and talk in general terms as a team, then talk at a deeper level with your bigger kids later. Be honest about what is going on. Natural disasters and other big crises aren't things you can shield your kids from completely, especially if their lives will change temporarily or for the long term as a result of what's going on. We can't protect our kids from the truth of what's going on in their world, but we also don't need to provide every detail. How much you choose to share with each of your kiddos is going to depend on them. This is why it's so important to really know your children.

Remember that younger children need more concrete and simple explanations about events while older kids and teens will need more detailed and nuanced descriptions. A young child can be told that, in the example of an act of terror, some people were hurt and killed, it's over for right now, the authorities are working to free and help injured victims, and the bad guys were killed during the attack. Again, this is highly dependent on your child's social and emotional needs. You do know best, so trust yourself. Your teen may ask questions. Answer them if you can, but remember that it is alright to tell your child you simply don't know and you'll keep them posted as you find out more information. Above all, reassure your sons, no matter how old they are, that they're safe.

If you're in a situation where you're not completely safe, don't lie to your children. Tell them what you are doing to ensure safety for the whole family and how law enforcement, military, rescue workers, and so on, are working to ensure community safety. When our state shut everything down and issued stay-at-home orders in March 2020 for the coronavirus pandemic, we assured the kids that we were all safe, together, and had things in place to be pretty self-sustainable for a while. When my husband would come home from grocery runs with stuff from the list missing or substitutions that were out of my kids' normal experiences, we explained things simply. "The store has plenty or food, but they were already out of the cucumbers you like, so Daddy got these instead. Remember that we have plenty of meat because we got that side of beef last fall and the poultry share from the local farm over the summer, so we'll be able to eat for a long time."

Find Some Normalcy

No matter how disruptive life becomes when tragedy or natural disasters strike, you can still create some normalcy for your kiddos to help them feel safe and secure. Even if you needed to live at a shelter for a time, you could still preserve some routines, like saying prayers before meals or bedtime, sharing a story or a song at bedtime, talking about the things you're grateful for, and so on. If you're home, try to keep up rules and discipline routines, but know that changes in behavior happen because your kids are uncertain. Now is the time for extra reassurances and cuddles. It's perfectly normal to expect your boys to be more dependent on you when something traumatic happens.

My kids were especially concerned for family and friends whom they abruptly stopped seeing during the pandemic. We made sure to connect with them via FaceTime, Zoom, and Discord regularly, and loosened our screentime rules so they could have more playtime with their friends in the only way possible. In times that are really tough, your sons will use up a lot of their resilience stores, and so will you. Do what you can to keep as many routines as normal as possible. Remember, though, trauma shows up in many different behaviors, including apathy, anger, frustration, withdrawal, and attention-seeking, among others. Be patient with yourself and your kids.

Be the Helpers

"When I was a boy and I would see scary things in the news, my mother would say to me, 'Look for the helpers. You will always find people who are helping.'" There is a reason this quote from Mr. Rogers is famous: There are always things that people can do to help, and there are always resilient people doing the helping. Encourage your boys first to look for helpers and focus on those stories. Then, brainstorm together on ways to help as a family.

As I finish up and polish the words in this book, our country is facing challenge after challenge. The division and tension are palpable. People have been on information overload for months and months, first with the worldwide spread of COVID-19 and then with protests and riots due to police brutality and racism. Families are scared and unsure of what to do, but there are plenty of stories in the news of people standing up for truth, fighting for justice, and helping those affected by the hardships and crises going on right now. Talking about those helpers anchors kids and gives them heroes to look up to. Our sons will cope better and recover more quickly when they help because it fosters a sense of control and builds self-esteem. Reading books to learn more about the history of our country, joining in peaceful protests or vigils, cleaning up businesses that were damaged in riots, bringing food or groceries to an elderly aunt who is too at-risk to shop for herself, or honoring someone who was killed or injured are all things our sons can do to help and learn in a crisis.

Our sons look to us to help them figure out traumatic events. They listen to what we say, notice how stressed we seem based on our body language, check to see if we're still following our same routines, and notice whether our tone or attitude is different when we talk to others from when we talk to them. If you need to have conversations with others that might be scary to your kids, consider doing so privately and not let your kiddos know you are talking secretly. Knowing you're talking about potentially scary things will only make their anxiety spike more, undermining the very security you hope to instill.

Unfortunately, there is no way to completely shield our sons from natural disasters, pandemics, terrorism, or other large-scale traumatic events. The way we react, though, and the support we can give them to offset the potential negative consequences of experiencing traumas make it way more likely that our sons will bounce back stronger than ever. Moms, the bottom line is that it's our job to stay calm and remind our sons that they're loved and safe. Remember that a strong attachment to their family–to you, mama–is the best protection you can give your sons, and it not only helps them recover from a disaster, but it serves them long into their future. Sticking together, minimizing the negative, empathizing, listening, showing confidence, and tuning into their emotions means your family won't just bounce back from hard times, you'll grow stronger than ever.

Takeaways

▶ Your job is to guide your sons as they figure out how to navigate what they can and can't control, so they can be able to regulate their own reactions as a result.

- Make it a routine to build up your sons' inner resources so they can store it for those unimaginable times that hit when we least expect it.

- Model stability and self-care while letting your kids and teens know that they're safe.

- In times of crisis, listening helps you become a detective.

- When you listen to your sons during a crisis, listen to clear up misunderstandings in particular so that they're not actually making a situation more frightening than it needs to be.

- There's no need to push kids to talk before they're ready, especially if you're clear that you're there for them and have shown them you're empathic and a safe space for them in the past.

- Younger children need more concrete and simple explanations about events, while older kids and teens will need more detailed and nuanced descriptions.

- Don't lie to your sons in an attempt to make them feel better during a crisis.

- It's perfectly normal to expect your boys be more dependent on you when something traumatic happens.

- Talking about the helpers anchors kids and give them heroes to look up to.

Chapter Twelve

Final Thoughts

*I take parenting incredibly seriously.
I want to be there for my kids and
help them navigate the world,
and develop skills, emotional
intelligence, to enjoy life, and I'm
lucky enough to be able to do that
and have two healthy, normal boys.*

—Joan Cusack

My ten-year-old Logan was sobbing. Her anxiety had reached an almost frenzied point over the last several months, making it difficult to know what would send her into a meltdown, panic attack, or withdrawal. Her routines had been severely disrupted, and she's also on the cusp of puberty, the new hormones flooding her system naturally affecting her moods.

This time her despair was centered around the loss of her favorite LEGO minifigure's hat, a teeny, tiny hat that was likely never going to be found since we have a dog that likes to chew LEGOs and a vacuum my husband spent an obscene amount on that sucks up everything in its path. I held no hope we'd find it, so I just held her.

Isaac, my seven-year-old who thinks the sun rises and sets with his sister Logan, came in and was instantly upset for her. He rubbed her back and asked her to tell him what she needed. She choked it out, and he disappeared. I heard doors opening and closing. He went up the stairs and rustled around the bedroom they share. He went into the family room, where they'd been playing LEGO together every afternoon. Finally, he went into the basement–alone, something he never does–and rummaged through all of the old bins holding seventeen-year-old Trevor's toys from when he was small.

He came upstairs a few minutes later with a handful of parts. "Logan, I couldn't find the hat Bob has been wearing, but this one looks just like it and was in the old LEGO bins. I also found you these three hair pieces and this cool LEGO cat. I want you to have my LEGO pizza too. I love you."

I'm humbled every day by my boys, who regularly show an ability to rise above challenges, show compassion, and hang on to their optimism and spirit in the midst of adversity. Are they perfect? Nope. Yours aren't, mine aren't. But I am positive that the kids who do the best through good times and bad ones are those who have deeply connected mamas like you, who give them the opportunity to stumble, fall, and get back up again.

Resilience is not perfection. It's not invulnerability. Even if you could, you wouldn't want to raise a son who showed no vulnerability. You wouldn't want to protect him from walking the harder road sometimes and standing up for good. For better or for worse, strength, confidence, compassion, perseverance, and empathy are most often fostered in the lessons our sons learn from the hard times. When your sons have the opportunity to go through these challenging experiences and show emotional intelligence on the other side, be sure to comment and compliment them on their sensitivity. Encourage their ability to nurture others. Point out when they become one of the helpers.

Parenting for connection before correction while building resilience creates stronger bonds between you and your sons, boy mom. You have a new awareness when you become a student of your boys, and that understanding promotes a deeper connection between you all. And, when you know them well, you can help them grow in positive and healthy ways. Not only will your boys thrive, your family as a whole will too.

Raising resilient sons isn't just about who your boys are right now. It's about who they will be in the future. It's about giving them the toolbox full of skills and resources that will best help them navigate all the ups and downs they'll face throughout their childhood, teen years, and adulthood. It's about raising the people you want to share the table with at holiday meals twenty years from now.

By using the strategies in this book, you prepare your sons to be better brothers, better friends, better husbands, and better fathers. For example, when he makes mindfulness and gratitude a regular part of his day and routine, he'll develop a much stronger understanding of himself, appreciate what is good in his life, and be in better control of his feelings and emotions.

Here's the thing, though: you don't have to become a perfect parent to make any of this happen. You don't need expensive programs. You just need to be present, active, and listen. Let go and let your kids explore, play, and connect. You will make mistakes. Mistakes are opportunities for you to show your sons that you're still growing and learning too.

I hope *Raising Resilient Sons* has challenged you to make small tweaks and implement strategies that will fit your individual child and your individual situation. And, when you come back to visit the pages again as your sons grow and change, I hope you'll be reminded how great a boy mom you already are and what you already know about parenting. Maybe it will empower you to tell me ideas I left out that might work better for your sons, and for others like them. You can send me your thoughts anytime through the voicemail or email contact forms on RaisingResilientSons.com.

Have confidence in yourself. You are the perfect parent for your perfect sons. Be courageous and trust yourself. Remember that *you* are the expert on your kid, not me or any other *expert* out there. Trust that, mama.

Finally, care about your sons so much that they never have to doubt their own abilities because they know you're always there to help them rebuild their resilience stores and inner resources when they need you. Help your sons know

▶ that you are crazy in love with them.

▶ they have unlimited potential.

- ▶ you'll let them learn for themselves that they control their world.

- ▶ the solution to most problems is within their grasp.

- ▶ they can be mindful and regulate their own thoughts, feelings, and emotions.

- ▶ they are unique and have individual temperaments, interests, and strengths, and you'll support them in all.

- ▶ you'll take care of yourself so they can see how to nurture themselves and other people too.

- ▶ that you work to make the world a better place for them and all kids, and they can too.

You were already the perfect boy mom the minute you held that tiny being in your arms if he was born to you, or as soon as you brought him home like my friend Aurie did with sweet Isaiah, the miracle kid. Your biggest challenge is still to come, mama. One day you'll need to think to yourself as you look up at the young man towering over you, "You can do anything. You are strong. You are resilient. You are kind. And, you can stand on your own." I'm getting there too. Trevor loves that he's a foot taller than me, and I mix up his and his father's voices when I can't see who is talking to me from another room. But he's strong. He can stand when he's ready.

So can your sons, mama.

So can you.

Additional Resources

Websites

Bounce Back Parenting
www.BounceBackParenting.com
Resources about developing resilience in kids.

Center on the Developing Child
www.DevelopingChild.harvard.edu/science/key-concepts/resilience
Harvard University's Center on the Developing Child site, with links
to resources about stress and its effects on resilience.

Hey Sigmund
www.HeySigmund.com
Site founded by Karen Young, Australian psychologist, specializing
in children with anxiety.

Raising Resilient Sons
www.RaisingResilientSons.com
The page for this book with clickable links to all of the resources
mentioned here, a book guide, free printables and activities, and
more.

Raising Lifelong Learners
www.RaisingLifelongLearners.com
The author's website, with resources, articles, and more.

Books for Parents

Anxiety-Free Kids: An Interactive Guide for Parents and Children, by Bonnie Zucker, PhD

Baby Signs: How to Talk with Your Baby Before Your Baby Can Talk, by Linda Acredolo, PhD, and Susan Goodwyn, PhD

Bounce Back Parenting: A Field Guide for Creating Connection, Not Perfection, by Alissa Marquess

Boys Adrift: The Five Factors Driving the Growing Epidemic of Unmotivated Boys and Underachieving Young Men, by Leonard Sax, MD, PhD

Boys Should Be Boys: 7 Secrets to Raising Healthy Sons, by Meg Meeker, MD

Building Emotional Intelligence, by Linda Lantieri

Confident Parents, Confident Kids: Raising Emotional Intelligence in Ourselves and Our Kids–From Toddlers to Teenagers, by Jennifer S. Miller, EdM

The Danish Way of Parenting: What the Happiest People in the World Know About Raising Confident, Capable Kids, by Jessica Joelle Alexander and Iben Dissing Sandahl

Deep Secrets: Boys' Friendships and the Crisis of Connection, by Niobe Way

Emotional Intelligence: Why It Can Matter More Than IQ, by Daniel Goleman

The Everything Parent's Guide to Emotional Intelligence in Children: How to Raise Children Who Are Caring, Resilient, and Emotionally Strong, by Korrel Kanoy, PhD

Free to Learn: Why Unleashing the Instinct to Play Will Make Our Children Happier, More Self-Reliant, and Better Students for Life, by Peter Gray

How to Raise a Boy: The Power of Connection to Build Good Men, by Michael C. Reichert, PhD

Kid Confidence: Help Your Child Make Friends, Build Resilience, and Develop Real Self-Esteem, by Eileen Kennedy-Moore, PhD

Knights in Training: Ten Principles for Raising Honorable, Courageous, and Compassionate Boys, by Heather Haupt

Last Child in the Woods: Saving Our Children from Nature Deficit Disorder, by Richard Louv

Make Your Worrier a Warrior: A Guide to Conquering Your Child's Fears, by Dan Peters, PhD

Parent Effectiveness Training: The Proven Program for Raising Responsible Children, by Thomas Gordon, PhD

Mindsets for Parents: Strategies to Encourage Growth Mindsets in Kids, by Mary Cay Ricci and Margaret Lee

Raising a Secure Child: How Circle of Security Parenting Can Help You Nurture Your Child's Attachment, Emotional Resilience, and Freedom to Explore, by Kent Hoffman, Glen Cooper, and Bert Powell, with Christine M. Benton

Raising a Self-Disciplined Child: Help Your Child Become More Responsible, Confident, and Resilient, by Robert Brooks, PhD, and Sam Goldstein, PhD

Raising an Emotionally Intelligent Child: The Heart of Parenting, by John Gottman, PhD, with Joan DeClaire

Raising Boys: Why Boys Are Different–and How to Help Them Become Happy and Well-Balanced Men, by Steve Biddulph

Raising Independent, Self-Confident Kids: Nine Essential Skills to Teach Your Child or Teen, by Wendy L. Moss, PhD, and Donald A. Moses, MD

The Self-Driven Child: The Science and Sense of Giving Your Kids More Control Over Their Lives, by William Stixrud, PhD, and Ned Johnson

Simplicity Parenting: Using the Extraordinary Power of Less to Raise Calmer, Happier, and More Secure Kids, by Kim John Payne, EdM, with Lisa M. Ross

Strong Mothers, Strong Sons: Lessons Mothers Need to Raise Extraordinary Men, by Meg Meeker, MD

The Whole-Brain Child: 12 Revolutionary Strategies to Nurture Your Child's Developing Mind, by Daniel J. Siegel, MD, and Tina Payne Bryson, PhD

Wild Things: The Art of Nurturing Boys, by Stephen James and David Thomas

Why Gender Matters: What Parents and Teachers Need to Know About the Emerging Science of Sex Differences, by Leonard Sax, MD, PhD

Books for Kids

The Absolutely True Diary of a Part-Time Indian, by Sherman Alexie

Ada Twist, Scientist, by Andrea Beaty and David Roberts

The Adventures of Beekle: The Unimaginary Friend, by Dan Santat

The Astronaut with a Song for the Stars: The Story of Dr. Ellen Ochoa, by Julia Finley Mosca and Daniel Rieley

The Boy Who Harnessed the Wind, by William Kamkwamba, Bryan Mealer, and Elizabeth Zunon

The Curious Garden, by Peter Brown

The Doctor with an Eye for Eyes: The Story of Dr. Patricia Bath, by Julia Finley Mosca

The Dot, by Peter H. Reynolds

El Deafo, by Cece Bell

Emmanuel's Dream: The True Story of Emmanuel Ofosu Yeboah, by Laurie Ann Thompson and Sean Qualls

Every Falling Star: The True Story of How I Survived and Escaped North Korea, by Sungju Lee and Susan McClelland

Fifty Cents and a Dream: Young Booker T. Washington, by Jabari Asim and Bryan Collier

The Girl Who Lost Her Smile, by Karim Alrawi

The Girl Who Thought in Pictures: The Story of Dr. Temple Grandin, by Julia Finley Mosca

The Girl with a Mind for Math: The Story of Raye Montague, by Julia Finley Mosca

Hatchet, by Gary Paulsen

Hope in a Ballet Shoe: Orphaned by War, Saved by Ballet: An Extraordinary True Story, by Michaela DePrince and Elaine DePrince

Ish, by Peter H. Reynolds

A Long Walk to Water: Based on a True Story, by Linda Sue Park

The Most Magnificent Thing, by Ashley Spires

Nothing Stopped Sophie: The Story of Unshakable Mathematician Sophie Germain, by Cheryl Bardoe and Barbara McClintock

Otis, by Loren Long

Out of My Mind, by Sharon M. Draper

A Perfectly Messed-Up Story, by Patrick McDonnell

Raymie Nightingale, by Kate DiCamillo

Rosie Revere, Engineer, by Andrea Beaty and David Roberts

Sad, the Dog, by Sandy Fussell and Tull Suwannakit

She Persisted: 13 American Women Who Changed the World, by Chelsea Clinton and Alexandra Boiger

She Persisted Around the World: 13 Women Who Changed History, by Chelsea Clinton and Alexandra Boiger

A Tiger Without Stripes, by Jaimie Whitbread

Violet the Pilot, by Steve Breen

A Visitor for Bear, by Bonny Becker and Kady MacDonald Denton

You Are Awesome: Find Your Confidence and Dare to Be Brilliant at (Almost) Everything, by Matthew Syed

Your Name Is a Song, by Jamilah Thompkins-Bigelow

Index

Acknowledgments

The future is a better place because of all the researchers, specialists, psychologists, and parents who have done the work to make the discoveries; about human nature and child development this book is based on, available to parents everywhere. Thank you to all of you who strive to grow and help parents grow too. Together we can raise a strong generation that is resilient, kind, and ready to nurture and love one another.

To all the people I have had the opportunity to learn from, teach, or get to know from near and far, I want to say thank you for being the inspiration and foundation for *Raising Resilient Sons*.

Having an idea and turning it into a book is as challenging as it sounds. The experience is both difficult and rewarding. I especially want to thank the people that helped make this happen. Thank you to the team at Ulysses Press for the opportunity to tackle this important topic and bring it into the world so quickly. The back and forth of hammering out ideas, details, and focus can be difficult, and I'm grateful I had the chance to have the guidance of Ashten Evans and Casie Vogel whose encouragement, support, and commitment to producing the best book possible was so appreciated. Thank you, also, to the design team and production staff for your tireless work in bringing a book to life that I'm excited to share with the world.

My poor, underfed, ignored children were subjected to the phrase, "I can't. I need to work on my book," so many times my son told me he "has no idea why people always talk about wanting to write a book, anyway, as it's not glamorous at all. All you do is close yourself up with your computer and other books." Thank you for eating endless meals of instant oatmeal, cereal, ramen, and frozen pizza. I promise I'll cook for you again soon. And thank you, especially, to my sons Trevor and Isaac, for letting me share your stories.

I couldn't possibly do any of the work I do without the best, smartest, strongest, and most resilient husband ever. This book was written during the hardest and most traumatic year we've ever had in our more than two decades together. We lost a beloved parent, had hospital ER trips for an unexpected illness, moved, sold two houses, endured a pandemic, and navigated many other family and work challenges on top of those big, traumatic, crises. Throughout it all, Brian, you were a rock–exactly the foundation the kids and I needed to hold on and be resilient ourselves. I've never loved you more than I do right now. Thank you for always believing in me.

I have so many amazing friends, colleagues, and cheerleaders that I can't possibly mention them all, but there are a handful that have shared stories of their sons and have given me so much support through this process and put up with hearing about the book again and again and again. Thank you Cheryl Pitt, Aurie Good, Shawna Wingert, Pam Barnhill, Cristy Stebelton, Jen Vail, Caitlin Curley, Kara Anderson, Alicia Hutchinson, Mary Wilson, Jessica Waldock, Josiah Smith, Samantha Shank, Erin Bozan, Kristina Berger, and Tara Williams. I love you all so very much.

About the Author

Colleen Kessler believes that you are the absolute best parent there is for your neurotypical, gifted, twice-exceptional, or otherwise differently wired kiddo.

The author of more than a dozen books for parents, teachers, and children, award-winning educator, educational coach and consultant, international speaker, and passionate advocate for the needs of differently wired kids, Colleen has a BS in elementary education, an EdM in gifted studies, and is the founder of the popular podcast and website Raising Lifelong Learners, as well as Raising Poppies, a community of support for parents of differently wired kids.

Recent titles include *100 Backyard Activities That Are the Coolest, Dirtiest, Creepy-Crawliest Ever!*, *Raising Creative Kids: A Collection of Creativity Prompts for Children*, and *The Anxiety Toolkit: 96 Ways to Help Your Child Calm Their Worries*.

Colleen lives in Northeast Ohio with her reading specialist husband, four delightfully differently wired kiddos, a pug puppy, a dozen and a half chickens, two red-eared sliders, and an ever-changing assortment of small animals and insects. You can find her online at RaisingLifelongLearners.com.